Research and Data Priorities for Improving Economic and Social Mobility

Erin Hammers Forstag, *Rapporteur*

Committee on Population

Committee on National Statistics

Division of Behavioral and Social Sciences and Education

Proceedings of a Workshop

THE NATIONAL ACADEMIES PRESS 500 Fifth Street, NW Washington, DC 20001

This activity was supported by a contract between the National Academy of Sciences and the Bill & Melinda Gates Foundation. Any opinions, findings, conclusions, or recommendations expressed in this publication do not necessarily reflect the views of any organization or agency that provided support for the project.

International Standard Book Number–13: 978-0-309-68962-5
International Standard Book Number–10: 0-309-68962-7
Digital Object Identifier: https://doi.org/10.17226/26598

This publication is available from the National Academies Press, 500 Fifth Street, NW, Keck 360, Washington, DC 20001; (800) 624-6242 or (202) 334-3313; http://www.nap.edu.

Copyright 2022 by the National Academy of Sciences. National Academies of Sciences, Engineering, and Medicine and National Academies Press and the graphical logos for each are all trademarks of the National Academy of Sciences. All rights reserved.

Printed in the United States of America.

Suggested citation: National Academies of Sciences, Engineering, and Medicine. 2022. *Research and Data Priorities for Improving Economic and Social Mobility: Proceedings of a Workshop.* Washington, DC: The National Academies Press. https://doi.org/10.17226/26598.

The **National Academy of Sciences** was established in 1863 by an Act of Congress, signed by President Lincoln, as a private, nongovernmental institution to advise the nation on issues related to science and technology. Members are elected by their peers for outstanding contributions to research. Dr. Marcia McNutt is president.

The **National Academy of Engineering** was established in 1964 under the charter of the National Academy of Sciences to bring the practices of engineering to advising the nation. Members are elected by their peers for extraordinary contributions to engineering. Dr. John L. Anderson is president.

The **National Academy of Medicine** (formerly the Institute of Medicine) was established in 1970 under the charter of the National Academy of Sciences to advise the nation on medical and health issues. Members are elected by their peers for distinguished contributions to medicine and health. Dr. Victor J. Dzau is president.

The three Academies work together as the **National Academies of Sciences, Engineering, and Medicine** to provide independent, objective analysis and advice to the nation and conduct other activities to solve complex problems and inform public policy decisions. The National Academies also encourage education and research, recognize outstanding contributions to knowledge, and increase public understanding in matters of science, engineering, and medicine.

Learn more about the National Academies of Sciences, Engineering, and Medicine at **www.nationalacademies.org**.

Consensus Study Reports published by the National Academies of Sciences, Engineering, and Medicine document the evidence-based consensus on the study's statement of task by an authoring committee of experts. Reports typically include findings, conclusions, and recommendations based on information gathered by the committee and the committee's deliberations. Each report has been subjected to a rigorous and independent peer-review process and it represents the position of the National Academies on the statement of task.

Proceedings published by the National Academies of Sciences, Engineering, and Medicine chronicle the presentations and discussions at a workshop, symposium, or other event convened by the National Academies. The statements and opinions contained in proceedings are those of the participants and are not endorsed by other participants, the planning committee, or the National Academies.

Rapid Expert Consultations published by the National Academies of Sciences, Engineering, and Medicine are authored by subject-matter experts on narrowly focused topics that can be supported by a body of evidence. The discussions contained in rapid expert consultations are considered those of the authors and do not contain policy recommendations. Rapid expert consultations are reviewed by the institution before release.

For information about other products and activities of the National Academies, please visit www.nationalacademies.org/about/whatwedo.

PLANNING COMMITTEE FOR WORKSHOP ON STRENGTHENING THE EVIDENCE BASE TO IMPROVE ECONOMIC AND SOCIAL MOBILITY IN THE UNITED STATES

Courtney C. Coile (*Chair*), Wellesley College
Wendy Edelberg, Brookings Institution, Washington, DC
Kathleen Mullan Harris, University of North Carolina at Chapel Hill
Trevon D. Logan, The Ohio State University
Fabian T. Pfeffer, University of Michigan
Mario L. Small, Harvard University
C. Matthew Snipp, Stanford University

Malay K. Majmundar, *Study Director*
Joshua Lang, *Senior Program Assistant*

COMMITTEE ON POPULATION

Anne R. Pebley (*Chair*), University of California, Los Angeles
Emily M. Agree, Johns Hopkins University
Deborah Balk, Baruch College at the City University of New York
Ann K. Blanc, The Population Council, New York, NY
Courtney C. Coile, Wellesley College
Sonal Desai, University of Maryland
Dana A. Glei, Georgetown University
Robert A. Hummer, University of North Carolina at Chapel Hill
Hedwig Lee, Washington University in St. Louis
Trevon D. Logan, The Ohio State University
Jennifer J. Manly, Columbia University Medical Center
Jenna Nobles, University of Wisconsin–Madison
Fernando Riosmena, University of Colorado Boulder
David Takeo Takeuchi, University of Washington

Malay K. Majmundar, *Director*

COMMITTEE ON NATIONAL STATISTICS

Robert M. Groves (*Chair*), Office of the Provost, Georgetown University
Lawrence D. Bobo, Department of Sociology, Harvard University
Anne C. Case, Woodrow Wilson School of Public and International Affairs, Princeton University
Mick P. Couper, Institute for Social Research, University of Michigan
Janet M. Currie, Woodrow Wilson School of Public and International Affairs, Princeton University
Diana Farrell, JPMorgan Chase Institute, Washington, DC
Robert Goerge, Chapin Hall at the University of Chicago
Erica L. Groshen, School of Industrial and Labor Relations, Cornell University
Hilary Hoynes, Goldman School of Public Policy, University of California, Berkeley
Daniel Kifer, Department of Computer Science and Engineering, The Pennsylvania State University
Sharon Lohr, School of Mathematical and Statistical Sciences, Arizona State University, *Emerita*
Jerome P. Reiter, Department of Statistical Science, Duke University
Judith A. Seltzer, Department of Sociology, University of California, Los Angeles
C. Matthew Snipp, School of the Humanities and Sciences, Stanford University
Elizabeth A. Stuart, Department of Mental Health, Johns Hopkins Bloomberg School of Public Health
Jeannette Wing, Data Science Institute and Computer Science Department, Columbia University

Brian Harris-Kojetin, *Director*
Melissa Chiu, *Deputy Director*
Constance F. Citro, *Senior Scholar*

Acknowledgments

This document summarizes the discussions and presentations at the Workshop on Strengthening the Evidence Base to Improve Economic and Social Mobility in the United States. Held virtually on February 14-15, 2022, the workshop was convened by the Committee on Population of the National Academies of Sciences, Engineering, and Medicine, and it was sponsored by the Bill & Melinda Gates Foundation.

This Proceedings of a Workshop was prepared by the workshop rapporteur as a factual summary of what occurred at the workshop. The planning committee's role was limited to planning and convening the workshop. The views contained in the proceedings are those of individual workshop participants and do not necessarily represent the views of all workshop participants, the planning committee, or the National Academies.

This proceedings was reviewed in draft form by individuals chosen for their diverse perspectives and technical expertise. The purpose of this independent review is to provide candid and critical comments that will assist the National Academies of Sciences, Engineering, and Medicine in making each published proceedings as sound as possible while ensuring that it meets the institutional standards for quality, objectivity, evidence, and responsiveness to the charge. The review comments and draft manuscript remain confidential to protect the integrity of the process.

We thank Courtney Coile, Department of Economics, Wellesley College, for her review of this proceedings. We also thank staff reader Anne Styka for reading and providing helpful comments on the proceedings manuscript.

Although the reviewers listed above provided many constructive comments and suggestions, they were not asked to endorse the content of the proceedings nor did they see the final draft before its release. The review of this proceedings was overseen by David Takeuchi, School of Social Work, University of Washington. He was responsible for making certain that an independent examination of this proceedings was carried out in accordance with standards of the National Academies and that all review comments were carefully considered. Responsibility for the final content rests entirely with the rapporteur and the National Academies.

Malay K. Majmundar, *Director*
Committee on Population

Contents

1 INTRODUCTION   1

2 SOCIAL AND ECONOMIC MOBILITY: STATE OF THE FIELD   5
   Introduction to Social and Economic Mobility, 5
   Key Findings from Sociology, 8
   Key Findings from Economics, 11
   Discussion, 13

3 CONCEPTUAL APPROACHES AND FRAMEWORKS   19
   Causal Inference, 19
   Integrating Intergenerational and Intragenerational Mobility, 24
   Interventions to Increase Mobility, 27
   Qualitative Research, 29
   Discussion, 30

4 STUDYING THE SPATIAL DIMENSIONS OF MOBILITY   35
   Research Priorities for Place-Based Investments, 36
   Studying Mobility in Urban Areas, 39
   Studying Mobility in Rural Areas, 42
   Discussion, 44

5 STUDYING MOBILITY BY RACE, ETHNICITY, AND
   IMMIGRATION STATUS   51
   Studying Mobility by Race and Class, 52

Measures of Structural Racism and Institutional
    Discrimination, 54
Studying Mobility by Immigration Status, 59
Mobility Among Asian Americans, 62
Discussion, 64

6   DATA INFRASTRUCTURE FOR STUDYING MOBILITY   69
    Administrative Data, 69
    Nontraditional Data Sources, 72
    Data Governance, 77
    Discussion, 80

7   MOVING FORWARD: THE ROLE OF POLICY AND KEY
    TAKEAWAYS   85
    The Role of Policy, 85
    Key Takeaways, 90
    Closing of the Workshop, 95

APPENDIXES
A   Workshop Agenda   97
B   Biographies of Planning Committee Members and Presenters   103

1

Introduction

Inequalities in income, wealth, health, and life expectancy have been increasing over the past several decades in the United States. Since around 1980, fewer Americans than before are doing better than their parents did—that is, more are experiencing downward socioeconomic mobility in terms of occupational status and income. A number of efforts are currently underway to develop evidence-based strategies for increasing inter- and intragenerational mobility and improving economic and social well-being in the United States. These efforts require an improved understanding of the factors that influence social and economic mobility, the mechanisms through which these factors operate, and how these relationships and mechanisms vary across and within different population subgroups. To this end, the Committee on Population and the Committee on National Statistics at the National Academies of Sciences, Engineering, and Medicine held a virtual workshop on February 14-15, 2022. The purpose of the workshop was to identify key research and data needs and priorities for future work on social and economic mobility (see the Statement of Task in Box 1-1).

Malay Majmundar, director of the Committee on Population, welcomed participants to the workshop and gave a brief overview of the history of the workshop. Members of the Committee on Population and the Bill & Melinda Gates Foundation had numerous conversations and exchanges about this topic, according to Majmundar. The workshop was sponsored by the Bill & Melinda Gates Foundation and an interdisciplinary steering committee was appointed by the National Academies to plan the structure and content. The objective of the workshop was to help develop an agenda and establish priorities for future research and data collections, said Majmundar, with the

> **BOX 1-1**
> **Statement of Task**
>
> A planning committee of the National Academies of Sciences, Engineering, and Medicine will plan and execute a two-day public workshop that will bring together an interdisciplinary group of researchers and other relevant stakeholders to discuss the evidence base on improving social and economic mobility in the United States. The discussion at the workshop will highlight current research and policy efforts and identify key knowledge gaps and policy-relevant research and data needs on, among other things: the factors that influence economic and social mobility, the mechanisms through which these factors operate, and how these relationships and mechanisms vary across and within different population subgroups (especially race and ethnicity).
>
> After the workshop, proceedings of a workshop of the presentations and discussions at the workshop will be prepared by a designated rapporteur in accordance with institutional guidelines.

hope of strengthening the evidence base for policy making and contributing to the efforts of broader communities of stakeholders, practitioners, and policy makers.

Kosar Jahani, a program officer with the Bill & Melinda Gates Foundation, introduced workshop participants to the foundation's past efforts in the area of economic mobility and opportunity, as well as the foundation's goals for this workshop. The foundation's work in this area is relatively new, she said. Some of the earliest investments were focused on research and data public goods, such as the Opportunity Atlas,[1] the Eviction Lab,[2] and the American Voices Project.[3] These projects, alongside others, have influenced how problems around mobility are defined and understood, said Jahani. These projects have also motivated a variety of actors, including government officials and local service providers, to think more strategically about the magnitude of the problems and how to address them in their own communities. The momentum created by these projects makes the foundation "hopeful about the power of data," and demonstrates how curious and compassionate inquiry can be a meaningful starting point for change. In this workshop, said Jahani, speakers will cover the current state of the field, identify pressing research priorities, and consider how to build the data infrastructure needed to support this type of research agenda. The

---

[1] https://www.opportunityatlas.org/
[2] https://evictionlab.org/
[3] https://americanvoicesproject.org/

foundation's hope is that the workshop will provide "ample fodder" to consider what types of questions should be asked and what kinds of data can be assembled in order to push the bounds of understanding some of the most pressing problems in the country today.

Steering committee chair Courtney Coile (Wellesley College) provided substantive context by noting that the workshop is occurring against a backdrop of escalating public concern about rising inequality in the United States. A mounting body of evidence points to high and rising levels of inequality, not only in income, but also in other outcome measures, such as wealth, health, and life expectancy. Coile said it has long been a "cherished American ideal" that hard work will lead to success and that each generation can expect to do better than the generation that came before it. However, for too many Americans in recent decades, these ideals are not being realized; in fact, she said, more Americans are experiencing downward socioeconomic mobility than in previous decades. To address this issue, efforts are underway to develop evidence-based strategies for increasing both inter- and intragenerational mobility. Coile explained that *intergenerational mobility* refers to mobility from one family generation to the next, whereas *intragenerational mobility* is mobility over an individual's life span. Creating these strategies will require an improved understanding of individual and contextual factors that can affect mobility outcomes including income, wealth, education, employment, and occupation, as well as broader factors like housing markets, family, neighborhoods, and communities. There is a need to understand the mechanisms through which these factors operate, said Coile, and also how these relationships as well as mechanisms vary, both within and across population subgroups. For example, research has demonstrated large and persistent gaps in socioeconomic status along racial and ethnic lines, which are carried from one generation to the next. Coile said that this evidence suggests a need for special attention to how experiencing disadvantages, discriminations, and racist actions within employment, housing markets, credit markets, alongside other arenas of life may influence social mobility.

To make progress on these important issues, Coile asserted, it is critical to know whether the existing data and research methods are adequate. Surveys, administrative data, and big data sources can be leveraged for novel empirical approaches; where the necessary data infrastructure does not exist, it is important to articulate what that infrastructure would look like and why it would be valuable. In this workshop, Coile said speakers and discussions would identify key research and data needs and priorities for future research on economic and social mobility. Rather than being organized by specific mobility factors or data types, the workshop was organized with the aim of identifying key issues that cut across factors and data types. The steering committee asked speakers to focus their presentations on future priorities—where the research needs to go, and what obstacles currently stand in the way of progress.

Coile outlined the structure of the workshop (the agenda for which can be found in Appendix A). The first session set the stage for the rest of the workshop by laying out key definitions and concepts in social mobility, and highlighting key findings and future directions. The next session explored conceptual approaches and frameworks for studying mobility, and the third session identified challenges and opportunities in studying the spatial dimensions of mobility. On the second day of the workshop, speakers addressed research priorities for studying mobility by race, ethnicity, and immigration status, and explored the data infrastructure that is needed to study mobility. Taken together, said Coile, these sessions provide a roadmap to the researchers who advance the understanding of social mobility, to the policy makers and funders whose support will be critical to address data infrastructure gaps and to implement policies to address inequality, and to the practitioners, who "bring these policies to life."

This workshop proceedings follows the general structure of the workshop itself; each chapter begins with key points made by individual speakers. The proceedings was prepared by the workshop rapporteur as a factual summary of what occurred at the workshop. The planning committee's role was limited to planning and convening the workshop. The views contained in the proceedings are those of individual workshop participants and do not necessarily represent the views of all workshop participants, the planning committee, or the National Academies.

2

Social and Economic Mobility: State of the Field

Key Points Highlighted by the Presenters:

- Social mobility describes how individuals move up and down the resource ladder during the course of their lives (intragenerational mobility) or in comparison with their parents (intergenerational mobility). Mobility can be measured by comparing an individual's origin and destination resource *levels* (absolute mobility) or *ranks* (relative mobility). (Deirdre Bloome)
- Useful data infrastructures for studying social and economic mobility must accurately represent the experiences of all population members and must contain multiple resource measures. (Deirdre Bloome)
- To move forward in social mobility research, it is critical to develop an integrated mobility model and a formal theory to support it. (David Grusky)
- Economic mobility research has measured the persistence of advantage across generations (intergenerational elasticity) and is increasingly focused on establishing causal mechanisms. (Joseph Ferrie)

INTRODUCTION TO SOCIAL AND ECONOMIC MOBILITY

Deirdre Bloome (Harvard University) provided an introduction to the topic of social and economic mobility. She began with a definition: "social and economic mobility capture the distance people move between their position in an origin resource distribution and a destination resource distribution, to help us understand society's openness." For example, she said, if affluent children become affluent adults, and poor children become poor adults, then income mobility across generations is low. Mobility has consequences for both individuals and society, said Bloome. An individual's movement out of poverty can impact a number of outcomes, from how many children they have to who they vote for. On the societal level, she stated, more mobility can: increase economic efficiency, innovation, and growth; shift who has power in society and reduce abuses of power; and increase the likelihood that people have the same prospects regardless of whether they were born rich or poor.

Bloome walked workshop participants through the concepts in her definition of social and economic mobility. A *resource distribution* refers to how markers of social and economic advantage are distributed among individuals and communities. Markers include income, educational attainment, earnings, occupation, and wealth; Bloome noted that these markers are related to one another but are not interchangeable. For example, workers with more education may be able to obtain a higher wage, which in turn may allow them to accumulate wealth. However, Bloom stated, in some situations, these markers do not rise and fall together. For example, groups with low labor force attachment (such as women in many societies) may have high earnings mobility but low income mobility if the way they replicate their advantages is through marriage more than employment. Since these markers are not interchangeable, she said, it is critical that data infrastructures for mobility studies include multiple resource measures.

Next, Bloome explained the meanings of *origin* and *destination* in the definition of social and economic mobility. The meanings of these words, she said, depends on whether they are applied to intragenerational mobility or intergenerational mobility. For intragenerational mobility, which captures change over the course of an individual's working life, *origin* refers to early career positions while *destination* refers to later career positions. For intergenerational mobility, *origin* refers to the parents' positions, and *destination* refers to the offspring's positions; multigenerational research further considers grandparents' and great-grandparents' positions as origins. Intra- and intergenerational mobility are related, said Bloome, but studies of the two are not exchangeable. The data demands are particularly high for studies on intergenerational mobility, which often require capturing long-term social and economic well-being with multiple years of data observed prospectively across decades.

Bloome used an analogy of a ladder to elucidate the difference between mobility, inequality, and poverty. Mobility is measured across time, either an individual's lifetime or across generations. Inequality and poverty, on the other hand, are measured as snapshots at a single point in time. Mobility is movement between the rungs of a resource ladder. Inequality describes the length of the resource ladder—longer ladders indicate more inequality (greater distance between the ladders' rungs) while shorter ladders indicate less inequality, with poverty represented by positions toward the bottom of the ladder. For example, said Bloome, a comparison of poverty between 1990 and 2020 would show whether the share of people living in poverty increased or decreased during this time. However, only a study of mobility would be able to determine whether the people who were poor in 1990 remained poor in 2020.

Bloome described two ways to measure mobility (the distance a person moves on the resource ladder). The first is *absolute mobility,* in which the destination resource level is compared with the origin resource level. The second is *relative mobility,* in which the destination resource level is compared with the origin resource rank; these ranks depend on whether and in which direction a person's peers are moving. For example, Bloome said, a person could experience upward absolute mobility and downward relative mobility if their income rose more slowly than the income of their peers. These two measurements provide "fundamentally different insights into the persistence of advantages and disadvantages," said Bloome. Relative mobility has traditionally been considered an indicator of equality of opportunity, because of its comparative nature. When relative mobility rises, she explained, people from low and high origin positions become increasingly equal in their chances of obtaining positions toward the top of the destination ladder. Absolute mobility, in contrast, has traditionally been considered an indicator of the extent to which economic growth is widely shared. In theory, everyone can experience upward absolute mobility if strong economic growth is distributed across the population. For relative mobility, in contrast, Bloome said, "for every move up the rankings, someone must move down." She listed some of the types of statistics that are used to measure absolute and relative mobility. For example, absolute mobility can be measured by the percentage of people who are upwardly mobile, or the typical gain/loss between origin and destination. Bloome explained that relative mobility can be measured by the percentage of people remaining in their origin quintile or occupational class, or through correlation between origin and destination positions.

With these definitions in mind, Bloome turned to consider how these measures help one understand a society's openness. High mobility in a society is an indirect indicator of high equality of opportunity. She explained that mobility is an indirect indicator of opportunity because, while origin and destination positions can be observed, opportunity is unobserved. Opportunity captures the destination distributions that might be possible for people from a given origin position, but equal opportunities are not expected to generate perfect mobility. Since some association between origin and destination positions is expected, some theorists distinguish between acceptable and unacceptable obstacles to opportunity. While this distinction can be useful, said Bloome, it is fraught with questions that cannot be answered empirically. For example, how should the freedom of parents to invest in their children's achievement (which is a freedom that leads to low mobility) be weighted against the freedom of children to not be limited by their parents' resources?

Bloome said there are three types of questions that mobility studies can answer: causal, predictive, and descriptive questions. Causal analysis can help one understand the processes that generate and undermine mobility, which in turn helps one understand how to disrupt these processes. However, she noted, mobility-generating processes are complex; change in one area may be undone by change in another area, and pathways stretch across multiple life stages and institutional levels. Moreover, interventions designed to alter mobility may not increase relative mobility if the intervention's impact is equal across the origin distribution.

Mobility can also be used to answer predictive questions, said Bloome, such as what will happen in the future given a certain origin position. Answering these questions requires good models of destination resource distribution at each origin position, she said, and early indicators (e.g., children's test scores) may be surprisingly uninformative about mobility because of the inherent complexity and multidimensionality of the pathways between origin and destination.

Using mobility studies to answer descriptive questions—such as how mobility in the United States compares to mobility in other countries—can "provide crucial stylized facts that help us understand our world and make decisions about how to act." Bloome noted that while people may have different opinions about what to do with this information, it is critical that they start from a shared understanding of the "ground truth" that can only be provided by careful and accurate descriptive studies. In order for data to be useful for descriptive studies, said Bloome, there is a need for data at the individual levels and data that includes all members of the population of interest. For example, if a study aims to describe people's destinations based on their origins, it should include people whose origins are relatively hard to measure, such as immigrants.

Bloome closed by suggesting that empirical work "must not shy away" from relative mobility, where movement up the ladder requires some privileged people to move down. Furthermore, she emphasized, empirical work must focus "with absolute vigilance" on providing accurate descriptive representations of the mobility experiences of all population members, including the most underprivileged members of society, who are often missing or underrepresented in survey and administrative data.

KEY FINDINGS FROM SOCIOLOGY

David Grusky (Stanford University) described five key developments in the field of sociology that have led to new findings and contributions in the study of mobility. First, he said, sociology is no longer laser-focused on class mobility, but instead has undertaken a more expansive examination of the many types of mobility. Grusky gave several examples of sociological research that demonstrates this expanded outlook. Paying more attention to absolute mobility than they did in the past, researchers have found a dramatic decline in absolute socioeconomic mobility, driven by declines in middle-status production occupations and an increase in low-status service occupations.[1] Sociological researchers have begun studying educational mobility in its own right, said Grusky, and found a U-turn in educational mobility that mimics the U-turn in income inequality.[2] While income and earnings mobility have long been treated as the "province of economists," sociologists have recently conducted research on topics such as earnings elasticity[3] and building a measurement infrastructure for wealth mobility.[4]

The second development in sociology, said Grusky, is a return to the field's attention to the demographic foundations of mobility. For example, Hout found a relationship between mobility and family structure,[5] and Bloome found that mobility increases as children transition more frequently into new family types (e.g., via divorce and remarriage).[6]

The third development is a shift away from descriptive analysis and toward causal analysis, said Grusky, with sociologists examining the causal effects of factors such as college and neighborhood. For example, Wodtke and colleagues found a strong effect of exposure to a low-amenity neighborhood during adolescence on high school graduation; this effect was particularly strong for poor families.[7] This is an area, said Grusky, where

---

[1] Hout, M. 2018. Americans' occupational status reflects the status of both of their parents. *Proceedings of the National Academy of Sciences, 115*(38), 9527-9532. https://doi.org/10.1073/pnas.1802508115

[2] Jackson, M. 2020. A century of educational inequality in the United States. *Proceedings of the National Academy of Sciences, 117*(32), 19108-19115. https://doi.org/10.1073/pnas.1907258117

[3] Mitnik, P., and Grusky, D. 2020. The intergenerational elasticity of what? The case for redefining the workhorse measure of economic mobility. *Sociological Methodology, 50*(1), 47-95.

[4] Pfeffer, F.T., and Killewald, A. 2019. Intergenerational wealth mobility and racial inequality. *Socius: Sociological Research for a Dynamic World, 5*, https://doi.org/10.1177/2378023119831799

[5] Hout, M. 2018. Americans' occupational status reflects the status of both of their parents. *Proceedings of the National Academy of Sciences, 115*(38), 9527-9532. https://doi.org/10.1073/pnas.1802508115

[6] Bloome, D. 2017. Childhood family structure and intergenerational income mobility in the United States. *Demography, 54*(2), 541-569.

[7] Wodtke, G.T., Harding, D.J., and Elwert, F. 2016. Neighborhood effect heterogeneity by family income and developmental period. *American Journal of Sociology, 121*(4), 1168-1222. https://doi.org/10.1086/684137

there is a lot of interest in distinguishing confounding selection effects from true causal effects.

With the emergence of linked administrative data, it has become possible to carry out high-quality trend analyses extending back into the 19th century, said Grusky; this new capacity to understand the long arc of history is the fourth key development in sociology. One example of this type of research is a study that found a sharp decline in mobility after the transition into a non-agricultural economy[8]; this shows the powerful effect of early industrialization and the exit of children from the agricultural sector on mobility, he said.

The fifth key development has been the rise of qualitative work in the area of mobility. Grusky shared a qualitative study on nutritional disparities in early childhood[9] that found that "low-income parents resort to unnourishing food because it is the main affordable treat at their disposal; in effect, it is an attractive way to treat their kids within the context of their budget constraints." He said that this work is a classic example of unpacking the social, psychological, and familial dynamics behind nutritional outcomes, which are critical for mobility. As further examples of the role of qualitative approaches in social mobility research, Grusky pointed to studies showing that that higher-income "helicopter parents" find ways to ensure that their children are evaluated well during primary and secondary school,[10] and that low-income students who attended elite secondary schools are substantially more at home at elite colleges than the low-income students who attended public schools[11] and "are left to flounder on their own" at elite colleges. These examples led Grusky to suggest that neither primary schools nor colleges should be regarded as "the great equalizer."

New Directions for Research

With these trends in sociological research in mind, Grusky turned to identifying new directions for research. His first suggestion was to *build an integrated mobility model*. Currently, there is a specialized research literature for each type of mobility (e.g., occupation, neighborhood), and while there is research that combines some of these types, the lack of an integrated

---

[8] Song, X., Massey, C.G., Rolf, K.A., Ferrie, J.P., Rothbaum, J.L., and Xie, Y. 2020. Long-term decline in intergenerational mobility in the United States since the 1850s. *Proceedings of the National Academy of Sciences,* 117(1), 251-258. https://doi.org/10.1073/pnas.1905094116

[9] Fielding-Singh, P. 2021. *How the Other Half Eats: The Untold Story of Food and Inequality in America.* Boston, MA: Little, Brown and Company.

[10] Calarco, J.M. 2018. *Negotiating Opportunities: How the Middle Class Secures Advantages in School.* New York: Oxford University Press.

[11] Jack, A.A. 2019. *The Privileged Poor.* Cambridge, MA: Harvard University Press.

model makes it easy to misinterpret the source of trends. For example, a decline in occupational mobility may be accompanied by a similar trend in earnings mobility; without direct measures of occupation, the source of the decline in earnings mobility may be misattributed. Grusky emphasized that the integrated model should do many things at once: model all types of intergenerational reproduction (e.g., education, occupation, class, earnings, income, neighborhood), integrate intergenerational and intragenerational mobility, include multiple generations, measure marital mobility and individual mobility, and represent assortative mating for origin and destination families. Estimating the model empirically with administrative data will soon be possible, he said.

Relatedly, Grusky's second suggestion was to *build a formal theory for the integrated mobility model*, with the goal of specifying how different types of mobility are affected by different types of human capital investments, and by predistributional, redistributional, and safety net reforms and changes. Furthermore, he stated, the model could show how changes at one stage in the model propagate to create changes at subsequent stages.

Another area with ample room for contributions, Grusky said, is *examining key inequality trends via intergenerational processes*. As an example, he pointed to the need for exploring the role of intergenerational processes in trends such as occupational racial and gender segregation, assortative mating, residential segregation, and life expectancy. There is also a need to *integrate qualitative and quantitative mobility research*. The typical approach, said Grusky, is to carry out two separate studies side-by-side, with the idea that they inform each other. However, he said there is no reason why these approaches cannot be integrated by carrying out qualitative and quantitative analyses with the same respondents, making it possible to directly address possible inconsistencies between these types of research. Grusky concluded that it is imperative that researchers *prepare for the big data storm* that will occur when linked Census data from 1960 to the present day become available.

KEY FINDINGS FROM ECONOMICS

In the study of mobility, economists were "quite late to the party," said Joseph Ferrie (Northwestern University). The earliest work on mobility came from sociology, and while two early economists dealt with mobility, they did so only incidentally, he said. For Karl Marx, mobility was a problem because it precluded the development of a stable class consciousness. In the 1930s, Frank Knight viewed the advantages that were inherited through families as an impediment to market competition. Even further back, said Ferrie, the writings of Alexis de Toqueville convey a clear sense that there was something "fundamentally different about the American experience" compared with European countries, as seen in the ease with which families could rise to the top of the economic system, and the ease with which families could fall from "prominence to ignominy."

Economists began to view aspects of mobility as part of the field of economics in the 1960s, as a consequence of urban unrest and conversations about persistent poverty across generations. The initial focus was narrow, looking at how people could move from the very bottom of the ladder to the "next one or two rungs up." Even here, said Ferrie, the interest in mobility was largely incidental and did not take a holistic view of the entire distribution or consider how mobility could be impeded or promoted at other levels. This research informed the War on Poverty, he said, but did not provide much in the way of an understanding of the processes of mobility from an economic perspective.

The first research that caused economists to "sit up and take notice," Ferrie said, was a formal theory of mobility by Becker and Tomes in 1979 and 1986.[12,13] This two-period model sought to explain the transmission of advantage across generations, looking at both unconscious parental investment (genes) and conscious parental investment (education). The model estimated an intergenerational elasticity of about 0.2, meaning that over the course of two generations, only about four percent of any advantage or disadvantage persists. This low number was "quite surprising" because it did not comport with people's "casual impression" of how mobility operated in the United States. The major flaws of this theory, said Ferrie, were its narrow focus on genes and education rather than other factors that can be transmitted across generations (e.g., social connections), and the fact that the model did not take into account that the timing of investments can be as important as the amounts invested. It is now estimated that the intergenerational elasticity is about 0.6 in the United States and above 0.2 everywhere in the world.

More recent developments in economics mobility research include reducing noise in the data by using multiple years of parent and child earnings, conducting analyses across multiple countries, and working with larger datasets. The early datasets that were used—such as the National Longitudinal Survey and the Panel Study of Income Dynamics—were often too small to answer some of the most important questions, especially with regard to mechanisms. Another development, said Ferrie, has been the progress on new metrics that address some of the undesirable properties of

---

[12] Becker, G., and Tomes, N. 1979. An equilibrium theory of the distribution of income and intergenerational mobility. *Journal of Political Economy*, 87(6), 1153-1189.

[13] Becker, G., and Tomes, N. 1986. Human capital and the rise and fall of families. *Journal of Labor Economics*, 4(3, 2), S1-S39. https://www.jstor.org/stable/253495

the intergenerational elasticity, such as mathematical issues that arise when a person has an income of zero.

In closing, Ferrie identified some of the most interesting questions and areas of current and future research:

- Can intergenerational mobility be accounted for solely by the relationship between parents and children, or do other generations matter? In trying to predict children's outcomes, for example, additional information can be obtained by looking at the grandparents' outcomes, even after accounting for those of the parents.
- Does inequality matter? What is the nature of the relationship between inequality and mobility? The "Great Gatsby Curve," for example, indicates that intergenerational mobility tends to be considerably lower in countries that have more inequality.
- For which outcomes (e.g., income, wealth, education) is persistence ("immobility") observed?
- Why does mobility vary across geographic locations in the United States?
- To what extent has mobility changed or stayed stable over time?
- What are the mechanisms (e.g., genes vs. environment, specific channels) by which mobility can be explained?

Ferrie noted that early work by economists on mechanisms focused on twin studies and comparing outcomes for monozygotic and dizygotic twins, and that some emerging research is being conducted using new tools such as genome-wide association studies, which allow researchers to look for genetic associations across generations in order to explain some of the correlations. This type of research has a number of downsides, said Ferrie: it requires enormous amounts of data, does not answer the question of mechanisms, and "basically has no policy implications." However, he said, it may help to narrow down the range of areas in which mobility really does change. While it may have promise, said Ferrie, it is too early to discern whether the promise is being realized.

DISCUSSION

Following the presentations, Courtney Coile (Wellesley College) moderated a general discussion with speakers and workshop participants. She began by asking the speakers to identify the measures of mobility that should receive the most attention. Bloome responded that "we always have to go back to our question." The measures researchers use depend on what they are trying to learn about, she said. For example, if the issue is how to improve jobs and the labor market, a focus on occupational and earnings mobility would be appropriate. If the issue is how to improve children's well-being, broader measures such as income and wealth might be more relevant. Bloome stressed again that measures are not interchangeable; for example, a person might have a high income but low wealth if they haven't yet received the returns on their investments. Focusing on only one measure "won't tell us the full story about mobility," but it can help focus efforts and intervention points.

Need for Integrated Model

Grusky said that there would be value in research that examines multiple types of mobility at once because it could help elucidate the driving force behind trends; for example, trends in income mobility might actually be driven by trends in occupation mobility. By working toward an integrated model that does not "balkanize the field into separate one-off studies," researchers could further the understanding of how types of mobility do or do not move in synchrony. Ferrie agreed that this is a promising area for future research, noting that it has been rare to have a way of observing a set of different outcomes within the same body of data. With new, more comprehensive data sources available, it is becoming feasible to examine multiple factors at once and to "feel confident that we're actually looking at different dimensions of the same problem."

Coile asked Grusky to comment further on his suggestion that researchers need to prepare for the "big data storm" that is coming. Researchers can prepare now, he said, by building methods to analyze various types of mobility all at once, and developing a formal theory for this integrated model. Bloome seconded the need for this work, saying that having a formal model to build on theoretically is important to help make sense of the empirical evidence that is evolving, and to consider how it might apply in different circumstances and at different times. To this point, she said, these theories and models need to incorporate heterogeneity in associations and causal effects across different times, places, and populations. "We know things will be different," she said, models should explore how and why things are different.

Using Mobility Research to Predict Outcomes

Mobility research is in some sense "inherently backwards-looking," said Coile; for example, a study can show how policies that were in place 30 years ago have affected long-term outcomes. In order to impact policy, however, researchers need to know what might happen prospectively if certain actions were taken today. Coile asked Bloome to comment on whether there are short-term outcome measures that might give clues about long-term outcomes, or if there are other ways to obtain forward-looking information from mobility research. Bloome cautioned against conflating ultimate outcomes with proximate outcomes, and advocated for an accounting of the uncertainty in the pathways between proximate and ultimate outcomes. From a predictive modeling perspective, she said, this means that models of both the variation and the mean, along with uncertainty in the prediction, are needed. For example, while on average affluent children become affluent adults, adult outcomes vary widely depending on factors such as job openings and labor regulations. Bloome also pointed out that researchers can leverage insights from machine learning in order to incorporate knowledge about variation and uncertainty into their predictions.

Timing of Measurements

In the general discussion, Michael Hout[14] asked speakers to address the issue of *when* mobility measures are captured, and how this might have an impact on the data. He noted that some types of measures—for example, educational attainment—usually end earlier in life, whereas other measures—for example, consumption—continue indefinitely. Ferrie agreed that the timing at which mobility is measured is an important consideration for studies, and that there are peaks for different types of measures. For example, income peaks in the late 40s and early 50s, whereas wealth peaks at the end of an individual's work life. This makes integrating different measures of mobility challenging, because it is very rare to have a dataset that includes multiple measures across multiple time frames. These types of data are becoming more available, said Ferrie, and it is important that researchers determine ways to conduct this type of integrated research. Grusky agreed that newer data sources will make real-time measurements across a variety of types of mobility possible, allowing researchers to get a sense of how mobility processes unfold over the lifetime and to identify and differentiate period, cohort, and age effects. Differentiating these effects from one another is important, added Bloome, because of changes occurring across society; for example, income is peaking later in life because people are getting more education and delaying marriage. Fabian Pfeffer (University of Michigan) concurred with the need to consider the temporal dynamics of mobility measures, both across the life course and across time. Having the ability to integrate measures of mobility across time would "fundamentally shift how we study social mobility."

---

[14] Chair, Division of Behavioral and Social Sciences and Education; National Academies of Sciences, Engineering, and Medicine.

Prioritization of Mobility Measures

A workshop participant said that the Bureau of Labor Statistics is planning a new cohort for the National Longitudinal Surveys of Youth, and asked speakers to comment on what kinds of mobility measures should be prioritized in new research. The participant said that this is a "great opportunity" to ensure that future data are as useful as possible. Ferrie said he would prioritize measures of health and social capital, in addition to the measures already collected. Bloome said it would be helpful to get information about the partners of the respondents, but that the most important thing is to not lose the ability to compare across surveys.

Family Structure

Two workshop participants brought up the issue of family structure and the importance of parenting. One asked for speakers' perspectives on how "non-cognitive skills" such as education, expectation, and self-control fit into the mobility picture. The other asked about the rise of single-parent families, its impact on mobility, and whether there are policy implications in this area. Grusky said that a full model of mobility would take into account both investments in cognitive capacities but also in non-cognitive areas. Bloome added that test scores are often used as early indicators of other measures, but they are often not the best predictors of outcomes. Other types of measures—such as non-cognitive skills—are more difficult to measure but may be more useful. Ferrie added that "we are doing a disservice" to parents by not making them aware that there are many ways they can help their children be successful. Even if a child's test scores are not high, "the child is not doomed to a life of failure." Rather than focusing on improving test scores, he said, parents should be made aware of additional approaches, such as those in the non-cognitive space. Grusky said that it is important to acknowledge that some institutions "illicitly select on noncognitive assets," and mentioned the college admissions process as an example. Interventions in this area are generally thought of in terms of generating non-cognitive assets on the supply side, he said, but they could also be directed at the demand side.

Regarding the question about single-parent families, Bloome said that rather than attempting to use policy to change family structure itself, policies should focus on supporting families with resources that will help children have the best opportunities. Family structures are changing dramatically and very quickly, she said, and it is unlikely that this trend will reverse; "people are making different choices and we have to respect those choices," she said.

Inter Vivos Wealth Transfers

A participant asked for comments on how inter vivos (between living persons) wealth transfers impact mobility, and whether researchers need better ways of measuring this phenomenon. Ferrie agreed that the transfer of resources from one generation to another is hugely impactful on mobility. These transfers tend to occur at pivotal times, he said, such as buying a first home, having children, or starting a business. Help from parents or grandparents at these stages "allows people to take a step up the economic ladder." It is essential, he said, to learn more about how both parental and grandparental resources impact mobility.

Measures of Subjective Status

A workshop participant raised the topic of subjective mobility, asking whether it was important to measure people's perceptions of their own mobility and social status. Grusky responded that many measures of mobility presuppose that people care about how they compare with others on a variety of dimensions, such as income or wealth. There are also measures that compare specific groups, such as siblings, peers, or neighbors. However, he said, relatively little is known about which type of mobility comparisons are actually relevant for the subjective assessments that people make. This is an important area for future research, he said, because there is good reason to believe that people's understanding of where they stand relative to others is important for their subsequent behavior. Bloome agreed with the importance of this research, and noted that survey data over time reveals that subjective standard of living has not been declining over time, despite the fact that occupation and income mobility have been. "This is a very important piece of the puzzle to understand," she said; disconnects between objective and subjective measures of mobility may have implications for people's well-being. Hout added that it is difficult for people to answer these subjective questions because it can be challenging to process inconsistencies in one's own status. While there are correlations between measures such as education, income, and occupation, there is also "an awful lot of play" when people are asked to sum up their overall standing.

Impact of Critical External Events on Mobility

The final question from participants focused on the impact of critical events—such as mass disasters or the COVID-19 pandemic—on mobility. The participant asked, "do we have the right kind of data that we need to understand the impact of these kinds of major events and craft the policy responses that might be needed to address them?" Bloome responded that measuring this impact requires "very fine-grained" data across time and space, which is becoming increasingly available. Critical events impact people differently, depending on their stage of life. For example, there is likely to be a larger impact on the mobility of people who were 20 years old when COVID-19 began compared with people who were much younger or much older. Impact also depends on other characteristics, such as being poor or rich, and it is important for research to collect multiple measures across time and space in order to fully capture the impact of these events.

3

Conceptual Approaches and Frameworks

In this session of the workshop, speakers discussed conceptual approaches and frameworks for studying mobility, and shared their perspectives on areas for future work in this area.

Key Points Highlighted by the Presenters:

- Causal mediation analysis allows researchers to assess mechanisms through which treatments affect outcomes. (Jennie Brand)
- A linked mobility trajectory framework can facilitate understanding of how mobility levels across the life course and intergenerationally are associated. (Xi Song)
- Understanding the social processes that give rise to mobility is necessary but insufficient for understanding how to translate this knowledge into specific programs and policies. (Greg Duncan)
- Qualitative research is essential for contextualizing big data. (Mario Small)

CAUSAL INFERENCE

In a causal framework of mobility, said Jennie Brand (University of California, Los Angeles), "origin" can be seen as the treatment condition, while "destination" is the outcome. For example, origin could be parental income, and destination could be the children's income. The causal framework extends most easily to a dichotomous treatment condition, said Brand, comparing "treatment" to the counterfactual of "no treatment."

However, mobility measures are not usually dichotomous, so researchers often use categories such as income quintiles and occupational categories. If five or 10 categories are created, the set of possible counterfactuals is quickly complicated. For example, comparing the bottom quintile with the top quintile may not be a realistic alternative or counterfactual condition. Income could also be measured as a continuous treatment, but here the problem of possible counterfactuals becomes severe. For example, it would be difficult to find a family for whom every income from $10,000 to $150,000 is a reasonable counterfactual to consider. Another challenge, said Brand, is the issue of selection. If there is an observed association between parent and child income, there is little basis for concluding that it is a causal association. There could be any number of pretreatment characteristics that impact both parent and child income. Figure 3-1 demonstrates this relationship, and how pretreatment characteristics (X) can be a cause of the correlation between incomes. These characteristics can be adjusted for using regression, matching, weighting, or machine learning approaches. If all known confounders are adjusted for, the association between parent and child incomes might be a true causal relationship. However, she said, there could be unobserved factors (U) that impact both incomes and bias the causal association (e).

A common research question is what role education plays in mobility, said Brand. She shared an "OED triangle," in which education is a primary mediator by which origins impact destinations (see Figure 3-2). Since paths b and c are strong, she said, education preserves privilege across generations and transmits social origins to destinations, thus playing a key role in social reproduction. However, education also facilitates equal opportunity to the extent that access to higher education results from factors other than

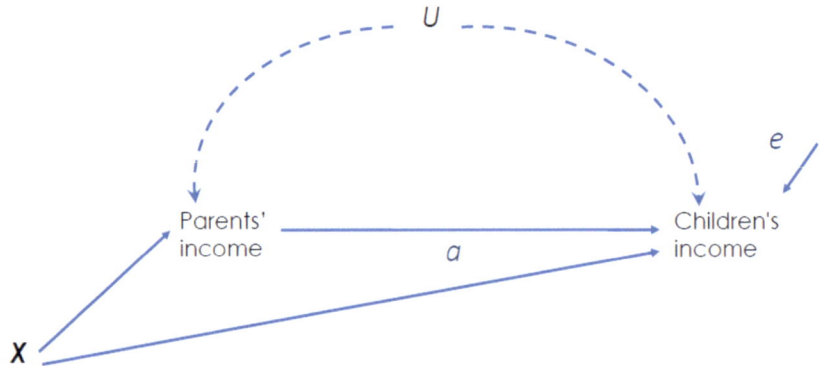

FIGURE 3-1 Effects of social origins on social destinations: causal association (e), unobserved factors (U), and pretreatment characteristics (X).
SOURCE: Workshop presentation by Jennie Brand, February 14, 2022.

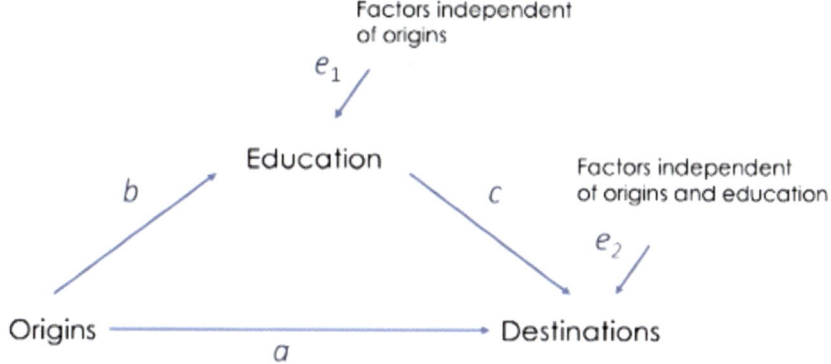

FIGURE 3-2 OED triangle: effects of social origins (O) and education (E) on social destinations (D).
SOURCE: Workshop presentation by Jennie Brand, February 14, 2022.

social origins (e1). There are large bodies of literature that aim to identify the causal effects of family background (e.g., parent income) on educational attainment (path b), and of education on destination (path c). Many of the same issues arise in this research as in the previous example, said Brand, in particular difficulty operationalizing education as a treatment. Researchers could examine preschool, secondary school, higher education, or any combination of these; even within higher education, one could look at college attendance, college completion, type of institution attended, or years of higher learning.

Causal Mediation Analysis

These paths can be considered using causal mediation analysis, which allows researchers to assess mechanisms through which treatments affect outcomes, said Brand. The goal of causal mediation analysis is to decompose the total effect of origins on destinations into direct and mediating or indirect effects through education. The mediating effect, she explained, reflects one potential pathway through which the treatment produces an effect on the outcome of interest. For example, early mobility research found that a college education mediates the mobility process and serves as an equalizer. This is illustrated hypothetically in Figure 3-3, where there is little direct relationship between origins and destinations for college-educated workers; thus, college serves as an equalizer. There is a stronger relationship between origins and destinations among less educated workers, showing that intergenerational mobility is higher among college graduates than among people with lower levels of education.

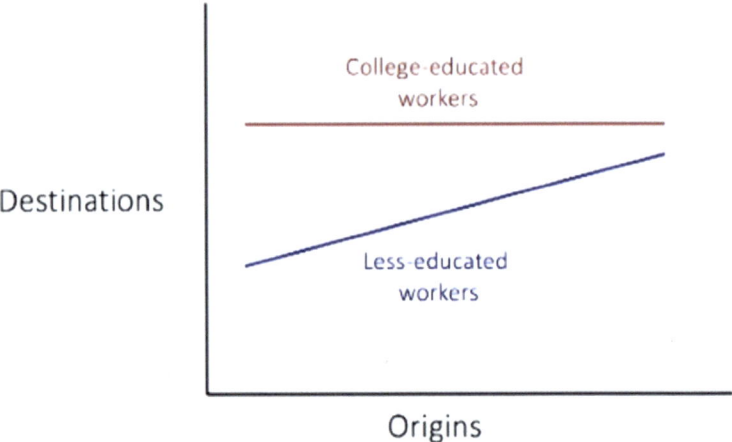

FIGURE 3-3 Hypothetical relationships between social origins and social destinations by education.
SOURCE: Workshop presentation by Jennie Brand, February 14, 2022.

However, according to Brand, recent research has questioned this relationship and has noted that the college equalization finding rests on an implicit assumption that the high mobility observed among college graduates reflects a causal effect of college on intergenerational mobility. An alternative explanation, she said, is that college graduates from low-income families may be more positively selected on attributes such as motivation than graduates from higher-income families for whom college attendance is a cultural norm. In this scenario, education is not only a mediator but also a common consequence of both social origins and other pretreatment characteristics (X); Figure 3-4 adds pretreatment characteristics to the OED triangle shown in Figure 3-2 above.

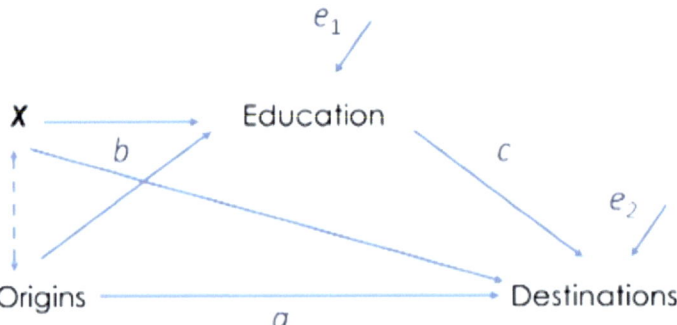

FIGURE 3-4 Relationships between origins, factors independent of origins (e1), factors independent of origins and education (e2) pretreatment conditions, mediator, and destinations.
SOURCE: Workshop presentation by Jennie Brand, February 14, 2022.

CONCEPTUAL APPROACHES AND FRAMEWORKS 23

Brand indicated that researchers have recently used a variety of methods to adjust for pretreatment conditions and to tease out the relationship between education and destination.

Heterogeneous Causal Effects

Another area of recent interest, said Brand, is looking at the variation or distribution of effects. For example, a researcher could explore how path c (education to destination) varies by social origin. As seen in Figure 3-5, examining the differences in destination between college-educated and less-educated workers at each level of social origin allows one to consider heterogeneous college effects. In this example, those with more disadvantaged social origins have larger observed returns from college than those with more advantaged social origins. This approach, said Brand, is useful for assessing how mobility processes vary across the population, and for attending to external validity. However, Brand continues, this type of analysis depends on researchers' a priori ideas of important sources of variation. Emerging machine learning methods can allow researchers to explore sources of variation that they may not have considered, and to identify subpopulations defined by effect heterogeneity.

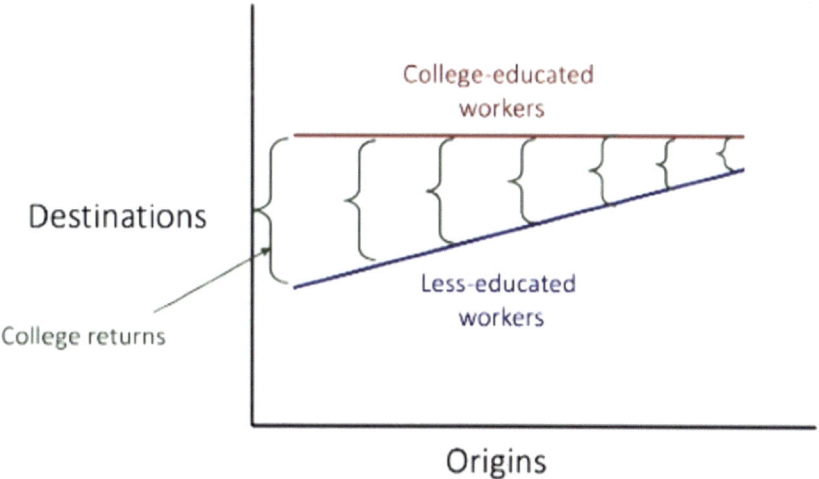

FIGURE 3-5 Heterogeneous relationships between origins, education, and destinations.
SOURCE: Workshop presentation by Jennie Brand, February 14, 2022.

INTEGRATING INTERGENERATIONAL AND INTRAGENERATIONAL MOBILITY

Traditional mobility research relies on single point measures in the parent and offspring generation, said Xi Song (University of Pennsylvania). However, parents and offspring overlap in their life courses, which means that transitions, turning points, and stages when careers develop may have implications for intergenerational mobility. Song presented two examples to demonstrate why taking a life course perspective is important for understanding intergenerational mobility. She began by explaining intergenerational income elasticity, which is typically assessed by regressing the offspring's log income on the parents' log income, and uses a static approach of either a snap-shot or a multi-year average. Figure 3-6 shows a summary of research; as the number of years averaged increase, intergenerational income elasticity also increases. However, said Song, much of the current understanding of rising intergenerational mobility may be related to the types of data and methods in use.

Song described a linked mobility trajectory framework that can further understanding of how life courses across generations are associated. Trajectories over life courses can be decomposed into four components: initial positions, growth rates, growth deceleration, and growth volatility. Using income as an example, initial positions refer to the income at the beginning

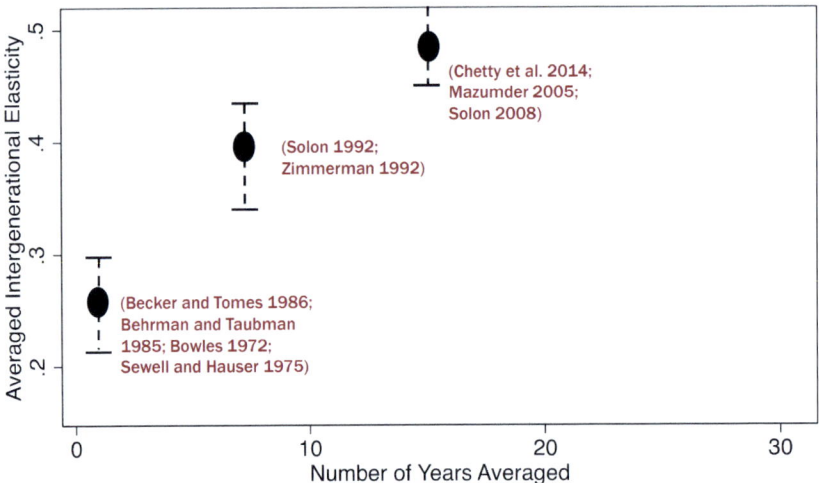

FIGURE 3-6 Intergenerational income elasticity measured by averaging over multiple years.
SOURCE: Workshop presentation by Xi Song, February 14, 2022.

of an individual's career. Growth rate is the percentage growth in income over time, and growth deceleration refers to a slowing of this growth. Volatility is fluctuations in income over the life course. A linked mobility trajectory framework allows researchers to consider correlations between parents and their offspring across all of these dimensions, said Song. She shared an example of a heat map that shows correlations between father and son incomes at different ages (see Figure 3-7). The heat map, said Song, shows the "long arm of childhood." The strongest association is not between the prime working years of father and son, but instead between the fathers' early careers and the sons' prime working years.

Song's second example of a life course perspective on mobility focused on the trajectory of income over an individual's life. A traditional mobility probability table can be used to show a child's chances of reaching the top quintile of the income distribution, based on his father's income quintile (see Figure 3-8). The highlighted column indicates a child's chances of success, namely the probability that a child reaches the top quintile of the income distribution.[1]

A life course perspective, on the other hand, Song explained, considers income quintiles as dynamic rather than static; people may belong to different income quintiles at different points in their lives. For example, Figure 3-9

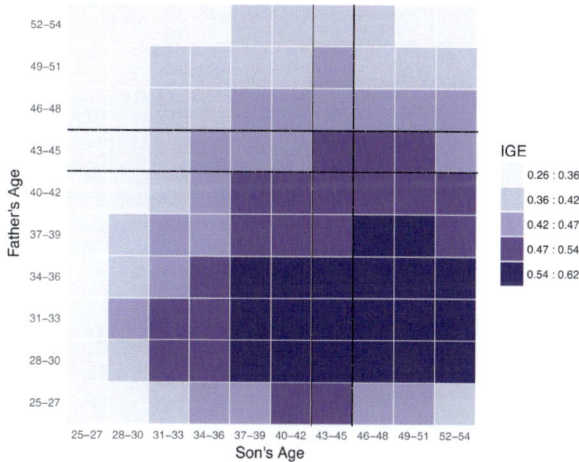

FIGURE 3-7 Intergenerational elasticity (IGE) by ages of father and son.
SOURCE: Workshop presentation by Xi Song, February 14, 2022.

---

[1] See Chetty, R., Hendren, N., Kline, P., and Saez, E. 2014. Where is the land of opportunity? The geography of intergenerational mobility in the United States. *The Quarterly Journal of Economics*, 129(4), 1553-1623.

		Son's earnings quintiles					
Father's earnings quintiles		1	2	3	4	5	Total
1	Bottom 20%	0.5	0.2	0.15	0.1	0.05	1.0
2	Second 20%	0.2	0.4	0.2	0.1	0.1	1.0
3	Middle 20%	0.15	0.2	0.3	0.2	0.15	1.0
4	Fourth 20%	0.05	0.15	0.2	0.4	0.2	1.0
5	Top 20%	0.05	0.05	0.15	0.25	0.5	1.0
		0.2	0.2	0.2	0.2	0.2	1.0

FIGURE 3-8 A hypothetical income mobility table.
SOURCE: Workshop presentation by Xi Song, February 14, 2022.

shows how different groups vary in both their income as well as the trajectory and stability of their income. Song said that, when comparing the mobility table to the income trajectory approach, the trajectory approach reveals substantially higher intergenerational association than the income quintile approach. This means that the static approach, which ignores intragenerational mobility, may underestimate the amount of intergenerational association. Parents and offspring may resemble each other, said Song, in both their level of income and also in the shape of their income trajectory over the life course.

Americans have experienced fundamental changes in their working lives because of rising inequality over the last five decades, and changes in the economic status over the life cycle may have intergenerational consequences, said Song. To better understand how these changes persist into the

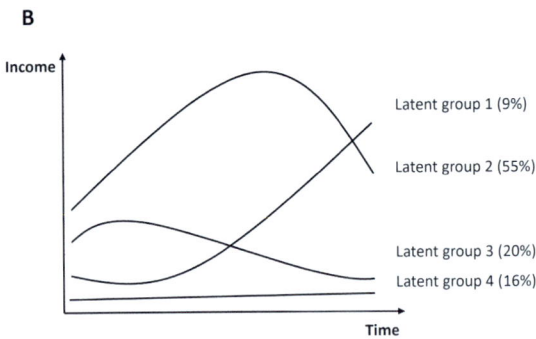

FIGURE 3-9 A group-based view of income trajectories.
SOURCE: Adapted from Nagin, D.S., and R.E. Tremblay. 2005. Developmental trajectory groups: Fact or a useful statistical fiction? *Criminology* 43, 873-904. Maughan, B. 2005. Developmental trajectory modeling: A view from developmental psychopathology. *The Annals of the American Academy of Political and Social Science* 602(1), 118-130. Workshop presentation by Xi Song, February 14, 2022.

next generation, future research should incorporate a linked-lives perspective across generations, among family members, or between individuals. This type of approach, she said, can improve understanding of how inequality is produced and reproduced in society.

INTERVENTIONS TO INCREASE MOBILITY

A great deal of attention is paid to interventions designed to help young people move up the mobility ladder, said Greg Duncan (University of California, Irvine). In 2019, the National Academies published a report called *A Roadmap to Reducing Child Poverty*; the report set the goal of developing policies and programs that could reduce child poverty by 50 percent within 10 years. This report gave rise to a new committee that has the goal of identifying policies and programs with the potential to reduce long-term, intergenerational poverty.[2]

Duncan began by describing the distinction advanced by Peter Rossi[3] between problem theory and program theory in the field of mobility. Problem theory—which the majority of this workshop has been about thus far—is understanding the social processes that give rise to the problem of intergenerational immobility. Program theory, on the other hand, is understanding how to translate problem theory into specific programs and policies. Sometimes, Duncan said, policy implications are included with a "throwaway couple of paragraphs" at the end of a research article. This approach is problematic, because program theory is a field unto itself, and even a deep understanding the problem tells you "virtually nothing" about what the best interventions are. For example, it may be clear that family structure is an important determinant of intergenerational mobility, but it is far less clear what policy makers should do with this information.

Duncan focused on the specific example of early childhood education (ECE) and introduced workshop participants to the Heckman curve (see Figure 3-10). This figure provides a visualization of the potential economic impact of additional investments in education; given the status of current investments, "where should additional money go that has the highest return to long-run human capital?" Heckman's hypothesis, said Duncan, is that investments in early childhood education have the "biggest bang for the buck," and the impact of investments decreases as the targets of the intervention get older. There is evidence both supporting and contradicting

---

[2] https://www.nationalacademies.org/our-work/policies-and-programs-to-reduce-intergenerational-poverty

[3] Rossi, P.H. 1987. The iron law of evaluation and other metallic rules. In J. Miller and M. Lewis (Eds.), *Research in Social Problems and Public Policy 4*, 3-20. Greenwich, CT: JAI.

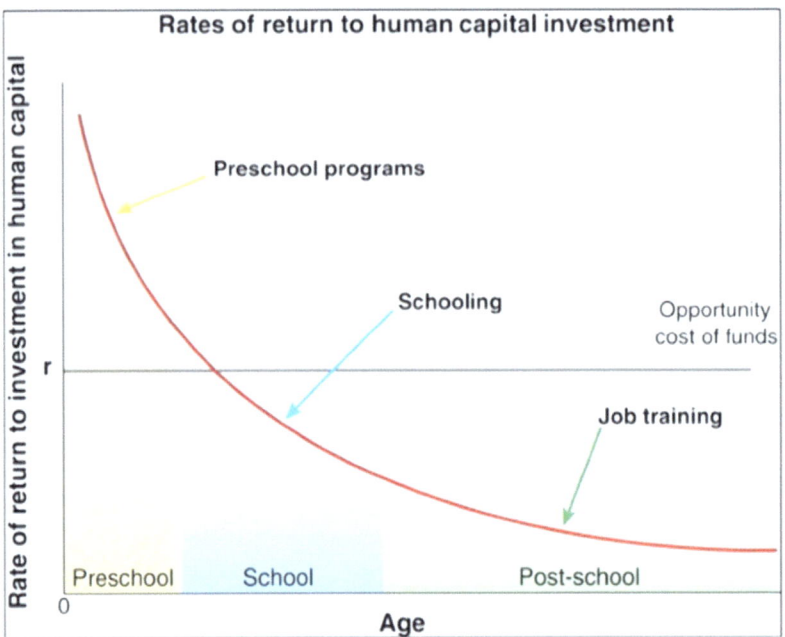

FIGURE 3-10 Returns to human capital investment by age of investment.
SOURCE: Workshop presentation by Greg Duncan, February 14, 2022.

Heckman's hypothesis, including examples of successful job-skill interventions and examples of unsuccessful ECE interventions.

Duncan delved into two older early childhood education programs as examples of interventions in this area: the Perry Preschool Project and the Abecedarian Project. He also shared data from a meta-analysis that examined the size and impact of the intervention at the end of treatment. The meta-analysis found declining effect sizes over time, even though, as Duncan put it, "you'd think we'd have learned something over the years." However, he said, it may be the case that "we know less about what the active ingredients were for Perry and Abecedarian than we think we do." Both interventions had strong results on longer-term impacts but differed in their pattern of impacts during childhood and adolescence. Moreover, both were quite expensive; Perry had $23,000 per child and Abecedarian had $105,000 per child. In program evaluations, it is important to compare impacts relative to the counterfactual, said Duncan. Many changes have occurred since the Perry and Abecedarian days, such as higher maternal education levels, older parents, and smaller family sizes. In addition, there is far more access to high-quality childcare now than in the 1960s. The point, he said, is that there is a much higher threshold to establish effectiveness for new programs and this may account for the declining effect sizes over time.

More recent early childhood education interventions, conducted in the early 2000s or later, include the Head Start Impact Study; it found positive treatment impacts for literacy but not math or behavior, and no consistent impacts once children started school. Other studies include the Tennessee Voluntary Pre-K program, which actually found negative impacts, and the Boston Pre-K program, which found positive impacts emerging years after the intervention. This is "all a big puzzle," said Duncan.

QUALITATIVE RESEARCH

According to Mario Luis Small (Columbia University), the emergence of big data is going to change the study of mobility and inequality going forward. As this happens, he said, it will be critical to use qualitative research in order to take big data and "produce good science from them." As an example of using qualitative research to complement and contextualize large-scale data, Small described research on access to banking in minority neighborhoods that offer services such as payday loans and check cashing. The institutions and services are easy to access, but the terms are often very undesirable—for example, a loan with high interest and a short payoff period. Proximity also matters here, said Small; the number of alternative financial institutions in a zip code predicts how frequently residents use them.

Small and his colleagues asked: are alternative financial institutions more accessible than traditional banks in minority neighborhoods? To answer this question, researchers looked at 19 of the largest cities in the United States and used Google Maps to calculate how long it would take to walk, drive, and take public transit to the nearest alternative financial institution and the nearest bank. Google Maps used to be an unreliable data source, he said. In 2008, Stacy Lindau and her colleagues conducted fieldwork in Chicago, in collaboration with residents of the community; the fieldwork involved walking the streets and counting the number of establishments on each block. They found major errors in Google Maps, with around half of what was on Google Maps not actually there, and about half of what was actually there not present on Google Maps. But thanks to crowdsourcing and improved data collection and compilation, Google Maps is now a quite reliable source of data. Small and his colleagues found that while there are more banks than alternative financial institutions, and on average it takes less time to get to a bank, there is an "enormous racial gradient." Among blocks with predominantly Black residents, about 40 percent have quicker access to alternative financial institutions than to banks. Among blocks with predominantly White residents, however, only about 10 percent have easier access to alternative financial institutions than to banks. The data showed, said Small, that "race matters a lot more than we expected."

In this area of research, Small stated, qualitative fieldwork is important for two reasons. First, it encourages the scientific questions rather than the available data to drive the approach. Second, it provides an essential quality check against large and "seductive" datasets.

DISCUSSION

Following the presentations, Fabian Pfeffer (University of Michigan) moderated a general discussion among speakers and workshop participants. Pfeffer began by bringing together themes from Song's presentation and comments made in the previous session about the timing of mobility measures. He asked Song to comment on whether her approach that looks at income trajectories across the lifespan could also be used to study other dimensions, such as occupation. Song responded that there are challenges to measuring occupation, including multiple categories, different definitions, and different approaches that would make it difficult to see trajectories. However, Song said that the life course also includes transitions in and out of the labor market, turning points, and other disruptions in careers; these issues have not been systematically analyzed but should be in future research.

Measuring Structural Factors

Pfeffer noted that many of the presentations focused on individual-level factors, such as income, education, and occupation. He asked presenters to comment on whether mobility research approaches could take into account structural factors. For example, fertility decisions can be seen as an individual-level outcome, but what is the role of the social context in which families raise children, and the educational and labor market institutions they encounter? And as another example, asked Pfeffer, what is the difference between considering race as an individual characteristic and considering the role of structural racism? Brand said that it can be difficult to capture structural factors in a framework that focuses on individual factors, but pointed to audit studies as an example of research that aims to assess the causal effects of racial discrimination. Duncan said that from the perspective of programs and policies, every level can be an appropriate target for interventions to improve mobility; for example, interventions could target individuals, family units, neighborhoods, or towns. Brand added that a causal framework usually relies on the assumption that the treatment of one unit (e.g., individual, family) will have no impact on other units; however, she said, people affect others in their neighborhoods and communities, and work is being done that takes the social context more seriously. For example, if many people in one area experience job displacement, this will impact the local labor market as well as the social and psychological experience of the workers. Small added two points about how a concept such as structural racism can be captured or addressed. First, research on the neighborhood level can help explore how race impacts the experiences or access of a community, not an individual. Second, racism can be explored at the level of institutions—for example, schools. Both neighborhoods and institutions can also be targets for interventions to address some of the negative impacts of racism, he said. These types of studies "can take a lot of the intuition that many of us have when thinking about systemic racism and make it a lot more empirically tractable."

Relationship Between Parental and Child Income

Duncan asked Song to elaborate on her findings that the early-career parental income levels that seemed to have the strongest impact. She said that they conducted further analysis to determine whether the age of the parent was the determining factor, or whether it was the age of their children when the parent was earning a high income. The researchers separately analyzed parents who had children early and parents who had children later, and found that the age of the children mattered most. This provides evidence, said Song, that age is actually an indicator of life stage, and that parental investment during early childhood development may have implications for future earnings. Michael Hout elaborated, saying that young people are very much affected by their parents' income while those parents are taking care of them, and that parental income when the child is older is less impactful. This points to potential areas for intervention, said Song; "if we want to reduce inequality between families and reduce intergenerational persistence of status, we should provide poor families with more resources during the early childhood of their children."

Role of Qualitative Data

Pfeffer asked Small to expand on his statement that qualitative research will become more important as big data become available. Small replied this shift will be necessary in part because big data are by and large produced by private companies or the federal government "for their own interests," rather than by social scientists trying to answer a research question.[4] When researchers take data that was collected for another purpose and try to make inferences about them, it is critical that they are able to contextualize the data. "The data alone can't give you the answer" to the particular scientific question, he said. The more researchers depend on this kind of

---

[4] Grigoropoulou, N., and Small, M.L. 2022. The data revolution in social science needs qualitative research. *Nature Human Behaviour.* https://doi.org/10.1038/s41562-022-01333-7

externally produced data, said Small, the more fieldwork will be necessary to figure out how much to trust the data and what can be properly inferred. Unfortunately, he added, training on qualitative methods is uneven and not always required in social science departments.

Impact of Unequal Distribution of Wealth

A workshop participant asked speakers to comment on how the "massively unequal share of wealth" might impact mobility; she asked if upward economic mobility might be limited by the fact that a small percentage of people hold a large percentage of wealth. Furthermore, said Pfeffer, how should this population with extreme wealth concentration be accounted for in mobility research? Pfeffer noted that this population is often not even part of the survey samples and therefore not included in most studies. Duncan replied that he is in favor of "heavy duty compartmentalization of the phenomena." While there has been a tremendous increase in inequality in both the top one percent and the top 20 percent, relative to other parts of the distribution, these groups are the product of very separate processes. For example, the rise of the top 20 percent is "a story of increasing returns to education, of deindustrialization," and other factors. Research is well served, said Duncan, by distinguishing between the top one percent and the top 20 percent. Given the massive concentration of wealth at the top, said Small, researchers should be asking "very different kinds of questions." This structure has consequences for taxation, resource distribution, and political leadership, which in turn have consequences for programs and policies (e.g., early education) that affect mobility. There is a need for research, he said, on the causes and consequences of this dramatic systemic inequality and how it impacts the population as a whole. Song added that many at the top of the wealth distribution are actually "working rich" (as opposed to, for example, owners of the means of production per Marxist theory), and so such extreme wealth concentration may be regarded as a market failure; if one wants to promote economic mobility, then reforming wage-setting mechanisms and promoting efficiency in the market need to be considered.

Future of Research

Pfeffer asked Song and Brand to offer their perspectives on where the big issues are in mobility research, and what lies ahead. Brand responded by pointing to three major issues. First, the conceptualization of the treatment and its counterfactuals really matters for identifying mechanisms and effects in a causal framework. Second, there is a need to use a framework that considers selection along the pathways; that is, considering pretreatment conditions that may impact an individual's pathway toward the outcome. Finally, said Brand, there is a need to focus attention on heterogeneity in effects across the population; mobility processes differ across the population and it is not always clear in which direction they differ. Song encouraged researchers to consider the dynamic nature of economic status over a person's lifetime, which may have implications beyond a single generation. For both research and policy, she said, the connection between current inequalities and past policies or social events needs to be considered.

Role of Mobility Research in Policy

For the final question, Pfeffer asked speakers to comment on the role of mobility researchers in policy. He noted that Bloome had discussed the importance of providing policy makers with valid descriptions of population parameters in order to ensure that the policy process begins with an accurate and shared understanding. In addition to this role, Pfeffer asked if there are other responsibilities for researchers to shape policy and conversations. Duncan responded that there is the potential for researchers to contribute to a better understanding of structural issues, and to point the way toward more effective, broader-based policy interventions. Small presented two potential paths for researchers, and wondered aloud which path should be taken. Building on the data that Duncan presented that showed declining effect sizes over time for ECE interventions, Small asked if the role of researchers should be to build on this evidence base in an incremental way, or to be more imaginative and think differently in order to "move the needle on inequality and mobility."

4

Studying the Spatial Dimensions of Mobility

As previous speakers discussed, place matters when it comes to economic mobility. This session of the workshop featured presentations on place-based investments, and issues and challenges in studying mobility in rural and urban areas.

> **Key Points Highlighted by the Presenters:**
>
> - While existing research establishes that place matters, a priority for future research is to understand why. This can be done by leveraging big data to measure additional characteristics of neighborhoods; studying the long-term impact of historical place-based policies; and evaluating recent and ongoing place-based policies, using surrogate outcomes to predict long-run impacts. (Matthew Staiger)
> - More policy research should focus on the active interventions that divide space and reinforce spatial stratification (e.g., home mortgage interest deduction, land use regulations, occupational licensing requirements, local housing decisions). Ethnography also has to be at the center of the effort to understand social and economic mobility. (Patrick Sharkey)
> - Rural areas are deserving of research, both on their own and as part of an interconnected system with urban areas. In order to understand mobility in urban America, it is important to understand what is happening in rural America and vice versa. (Daniel Lichter)

RESEARCH PRIORITIES FOR PLACE-BASED INVESTMENTS

Rates of economic mobility vary drastically across different regions of the United States, said Matthew Staiger (Harvard University, Opportunity Insights). Staiger shared a map from the Opportunity Atlas, which shows the income of adults who were born into low-income families (see Figure 4-1). The red- and orange-shaded areas are areas of low economic mobility, whereas blue and green represent areas of high economic mobility. For example, he said, a child who grows up in a low-income family in Charlotte, North Carolina, has an expected annual income of $26,000 at age 35. A similar child growing up in Dubuque, Iowa, is expected to make almost twice that, earning $46,000 per year at age 35. Staiger said that a better understanding of why these disparities exist may enable improved outcomes for some children.

These disparities also exist at the hyperlocal level, he said. For example, in Brooklyn, New York, Black children from low-income families who were born on the north side of Dumont Avenue have an expected income of about $17,000 at age 35, while Black children born on the south side of the street are expected to make almost $10,000 more. The key takeaway from these data, said Staiger, is that there may be scope for policies to operate at a neighborhood level, rather than a city or regional level. Based on this evidence, there are two broad strategies for increasing economic opportunity, said Staiger. The first is to reduce segregation and reduce barriers that prevent low-income families from accessing and moving to high-opportunity neighborhoods. The second is to use place-based investments to increase upward mobility in low-opportunity neighborhoods; that is, bring economic opportunity to where people are already living. Staiger focused the remainder of his presentation on place-based investments, considering three central questions:

- What are the mechanisms through which neighborhoods shape economic opportunity?
- What are the causal impacts of historical place-based investments?
- Can researchers predict long-run impacts of current interventions more quickly?

The current state of the literature has shown convincingly that where a child grows up matters greatly for long-run outcomes, said Staiger, but much less is known about why that is the case. To better understand the mechanisms that shape mobility by place, Staiger and his colleagues are gathering data on additional characteristics of neighborhoods. One project is using social media data in order to construct neighborhood-level measures of social networks; this will allow researchers to relate measures of

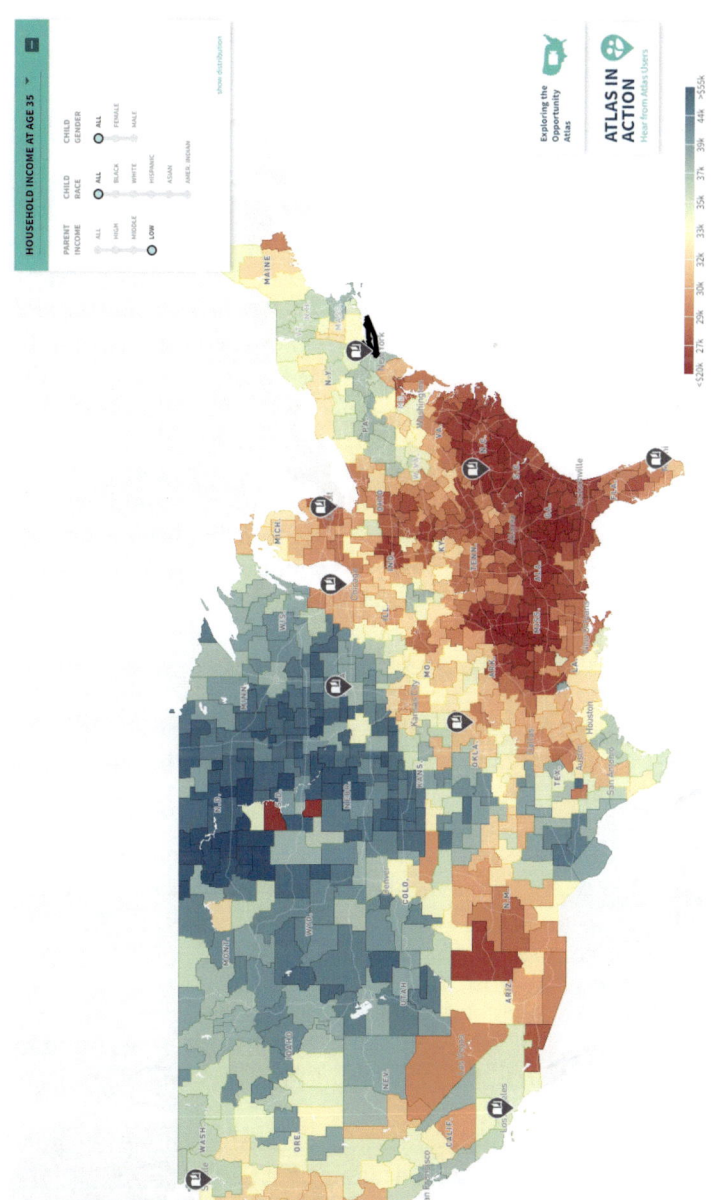

FIGURE 4-1 Rates of economic mobility in the United States.
SOURCE: Workshop presentation by Matthew Staiger, February 14, 2022. https://www.opportunityatlas.org

social network to measures of economic mobility. The second project is using data from the Social Security Administration to create measures of life expectancy at the neighborhood level, with subgroups defined by sex, race, and income.

Staiger offered his perspective on where future research in this area should go. There is a great deal to be learned, he said, by constructing additional measures of both the characteristics of neighborhoods and the outcomes of its residents. For example, area-based measures could include crime, policing, discrimination, pollution, access to credit, and substance abuse. This is an area with enormous potential for using big data from private companies alongside some of the more traditional data sources, such as administrative sources or survey data. With these new measures in hand, said Staiger, there are two approaches for better understanding the mechanisms of mobility. The first is to compare the characteristics between high- and low-opportunity neighborhoods, and the second is to look across time in a given neighborhood. For example, if the crime rates decline in a neighborhood, is this decline associated with better life prospects for the children growing up there? One way to study changes across time is to look at past policies or programs that were targeted at neighborhoods; there is "great value" in fully evaluating the impact of historical place-based investments in order to understand who was affected and how.

Current understanding of the impact of place-based policies is incomplete, Staiger said, in large part because of significant data hurdles. He shared an example of his work in order to illuminate the issues with data. A federal program called HOPE VI provided almost $7 billion in order to improve the living conditions of distressed public housing projects in the 1990s and 2000s. One specific project, he said, was a $20 million grant to the Dixie Homes Projects in Memphis, Tennessee. The neighborhood was characterized by very high poverty rates and very high crime rates, and it was isolated from the rest of the city by the layout of buildings and roads. The grant money was used to demolish old buildings and construct new buildings that would house both public housing residents and people paying market prices, with the intent of transforming the neighborhood into a mixed-income community. The program had a massive impact on the characteristics of the neighborhood, said Staiger, with the poverty rate dropping from 80 percent in 2000 to 20 percent in 2017. However, he said, what is not clear is who benefited from the program and how. To the extent that the program simply displaced existing residents into other high-poverty neighborhoods, those residents were unlikely to have benefitted.

In order to understand the impact of these types of programs at an individual level, two kinds of data are needed: big data to observe most of the people in the geographic area, and data with longitudinal linkages to follow people if they move out of the area. In the current project, said Staiger, these data hurdles have been addressed by using a combination of tax records, administrative records, Census survey records, and private company data. Another project that is aimed at building data infrastructure is working to link historical Census data to tax records. These datasets, said Staiger, will ideally provide both the large sample sizes and longitudinal linkages that are critical for evaluating place-based policies.

In addition to evaluating historical place-based programs, future research should prioritize tracking and monitoring the impact of current policies, said Staiger. Many place-based policies are motivated in part by a desire to improve the life prospects of children growing up in the targeted area, he said, and it would be useful to be able to evaluate the efficacy of the programs "without having to wait several decades for the children to grow up." Short-run outcomes could be identified that would allow researchers to forecast long-run outcomes. An example of this kind of work is a project that looks at older research on charter schools in order to link short-run outcomes, such as test scores, with long-run outcomes. If successful, this approach will allow researchers to use the methods developed in order to evaluate and anticipate the long-run outcomes of current policies. Building a broader set of these types of intermediate or surrogate outcomes to predict long-run outcomes, said Staiger, will be very useful for evaluating policies and programs in real time.

STUDYING MOBILITY IN URBAN AREAS

It is clear that space is directly and causally related to prospects for economic and social mobility, said Patrick Sharkey (Princeton University). He offered three statements that drill down into this overarching idea and that have implications for both understanding mobility and interventions directed at mobility:

- Spatial advantages and disadvantages are long-term multigenerational processes;
- Spatial inequality is generated by active interventions into space; and
- Mobility happens through processes that can be captured by ethnography: interactions, local social processes, turning points, shifts in mindset, and sense of identity.

Long-Term and Multigenerational Processes

Most of the literature on neighborhood effects—that is, the relationship between where young people spend their childhoods and where they end up—examines the neighborhood environment for only one or two years. However, said Sharkey, this does not capture the full experience of spatial advantage or disadvantage. He shared a figure that shows that about half of Black Americans in the United States have lived in the poorest quarter of U.S. neighborhoods for multiple, consecutive generations (see Figure 4-2). This experience, he said, is extremely rare for White families in the United States, and is not explained by economic characteristics or anything observable in the data. Instead, the combination of social policies and the persistence of segregation has led to these severe racial inequalities in neighborhood environments. The persistence of spatial inequality by race is directly linked with prospects for economic mobility, said Sharkey. For example, among families who are exposed to disadvantaged environments, downward mobility is much more common among Black Americans than among White Americans. Sharkey identified some of the implications of the fact that mobility is linked to long-term and multigenerational processes. First, he said, places—including institutions, exposures, and opportunities—are central to the mobility process. Second, understanding the histories of places and people is essential to understanding social and economic mobility. Third, to understand inequality today, research must be prioritized that links areas, people, and families across long periods of time and across regions and countries. For more information in this area,

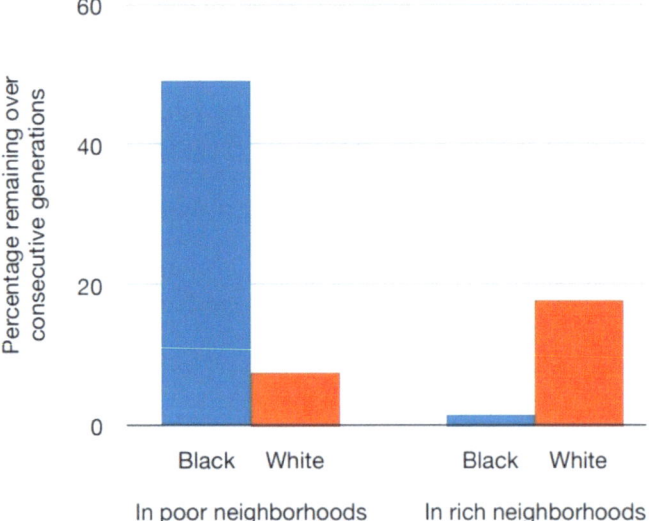

FIGURE 4-2 Racial differences in persistence in living in rich or poor neighborhoods across generations.
SOURCE: Sharkey, P. 2013. *Stuck in Place: Urban Neighborhoods and the End of Progress toward Racial Equality*. Chicago, IL: University of Chicago Press.

Sharkey recommended that interested workshop participants read historical work by Rothstein[1] and Derenoncourt.[2]

Active Interventions

Conversations about policy are often focused on programs that have the potential to reduce inequality and enhance mobility, said Sharkey. Often not discussed, however, are policy interventions that play a role in creating or reinforcing spatial inequality and reducing mobility. There are two dominant approaches to improving mobility for people in poor neighborhoods: helping them move to other neighborhoods or investing in disadvantaged areas. However, a third approach, said Sharkey, is to end the interventions that have been implemented over time to create and reinforce inequality. For example, redlining and yellow-lining have been found to have long-term consequences for economic mobility. Sharkey shared an example from Atlanta, where "urban renewal" policies resulted in a reshaped city, with interstate highways connecting the suburbs to the central city, suburbs zoned for single-family housing, and highways built in ways that reinforced the boundaries between Black and White neighborhoods. "It's not an accident," said Sharkey, that children growing up in some Atlanta suburbs will grow up to make significantly more than children growing up in neighborhoods on the other side of the river. This inequality "is the result of active intervention into urban space, with the goal of dividing space, in order to hoard resources, in order to exclude disadvantaged populations, in order to reinforce spatial inequality."

When researchers acknowledge that spatial inequalities are generated by active interventions in the space, said Sharkey, it becomes clear that inequality is relational; the decisions made by actors on one side of a boundary affect the outcomes on the other side of the boundary. Neighborhoods are not islands, but are part of social systems of advantage and disadvantage. There is a need for policy research that focuses on active interventions to divide space and reinforce spatial stratification, such as land use regulations, occupational licensing requirements, and local housing decisions, said Sharkey. "We don't just need programs to help people move across boundaries [but need to] know why those boundaries are there to begin with." To develop interventions that will have a long-term capacity to reduce spatial inequality and enhance mobility, he said, there is a need to demolish the boundaries drawn by current and past interventions.

---

[1] Rothstein, R. 2017. *The Color of Law: A Forgotten History of How Our Government Segregated America.* New York: Liveright.
[2] Derenoncourt, E. 2022. Can you move to opportunity? Evidence from the great migration. *American Economic Review, 112*(2), 369-408.

The Role of Ethnography

Economic and social mobility happen through processes that occur on the ground and in real time, said Sharkey, including interactions, local social processes, turning points in lives, shifts in mindset, identity formation, and networks. These are processes that are difficult to capture in large-scale big data, he said, but can be examined through ethnography. For example, he said, research has demonstrated that community violence is a central factor in the process of economic and social mobility. In 2020, violence rose in nearly all big cities and skyrocketed in some. Sharkey said that he was frequently asked to comment on what was happening, and he said he "didn't have a great answer." There was a need for ethnographic studies to examine, in real-time, factors such as changes to the local social order, the way police interact with residents, and the mindset and choices of young people. Ethnography must be at the center of the effort to understand social and economic mobility, said Sharkey; he pointed to the American Voices project as an example of the type of continuous fieldwork that needs to become more common.

STUDYING MOBILITY IN RURAL AREAS

As other speakers have noted, said Daniel Lichter (Cornell University), where you live matters—and this is true in rural areas as well. Unfortunately, he said, there has not been a great deal of attention on mobility in rural areas. An urban-centric view tends to dominate, with a lot of attention on poor children in big cities. However, systemic and institutional racism is pervasive and obvious in the "invisible places" in rural America—for example, the South's rural Black Belt, the lower Rio Grande valley, or on Indian reservations. Rural segregation and geographic isolation in these areas are a direct result of the historical legacy of slavery, racial oppression, land grabs, conflict, and violence, and the effects persist to this day. Lichter emphasized that rural and urban areas and populations are not opposite or isolated from one another, but instead are interconnected and interface in multiple ways. In order to understand mobility in urban America, he said, you have to understand what is happening in rural America and vice versa.

It is critical to include rural America to ensure a spatially inclusive approach to studying social mobility, said Lichter. Fortunately, recent signs suggest that rural areas are on America's political and legislative policy agenda; for example, a recent Brookings Institution report on reimagining rural policy[3] and an Urban Institute report on defining rural areas for hu-

---

[3] https://www.brookings.edu/research/reimagining-rural-policy-organizing-federal-assistance-to-maximize-rural-prosperity/

man services delivery.[4] He identified a number of reasons for this growing attention on rural issues. First, there has been an increased interest in understanding the "disaffected, resentful, forgotten rural voters" who voted for Trump. Second, there is growing rural-urban inequality, with growing differences in concentrated poverty, intergenerational poverty, employment, family patterns, health outcomes, and life expectancy. Lichter gave several examples of these changes in rural areas, including increases in marital and family instability, reduction in access to abortion and contraception, and growth of unemployment and underemployment. The third reason for increased attention to rural areas, said Lichter, is the "3 Ds" of depopulation, death, and diversity: the population of rural America has declined over the past decade; "deaths of despair" are increasingly common; and a majority of the population growth over the last decade is from groups other than non-Hispanic White people.

The research community, said Lichter, "must work toward mainstreaming rural-oriented work as opposed to relegating it to the backwater as unimportant or, worse, falling prey to conventional stereotypes about rural people and places." Research on rural America needs to acknowledge and examine the heterogeneity among communities, he added, sharing an old saying in the field of rural sociology: "When you've seen one rural community, you've seen one rural community." In addition, the boundaries that separate rural and urban America are "fluid and ambiguous," and research should examine the ways that urban and rural areas are interconnected in the world. Lichter noted that in universities, people who study rural areas are often isolated from other researchers, and there is a difference in status and resources allocated. He emphasized the need for researchers to bridge this divide and to study the rural-urban interface.[5]

Despite the growing need for research in rural areas, said Lichter, there are a number of data challenges. The first overarching issue, he said, is imprecise estimates due to a lack of sufficient data. This issue is caused by a variety of factors, including small numbers of participants in research, data suppression in Census data (especially for minority populations), rural heterogeneity, difficulty with tracking and retention as respondents move, and a lack of personnel and infrastructure to deal with big data. The second major challenge, said Lichter, is rural measurement; in particular, defining the term *rural*. In the 1960s, the Economic Research Service developed the rural-urban continuum code to categorize areas where people lived. Today, many of these categories no longer apply or no longer predict the types

---

[4] https://www.urban.org/research/publication/defining-rural-study-human-services-programs-rural-contexts

[5] Lichter, D.T., and Brown, D.L. 2014. The new rural-urban interface: Lessons for higher education. *Choices*, Quarter 1.

of outcomes that are common in particularly rural areas. The government uses core-based units to define non-metropolitan areas, which includes small towns and the open countryside. However, the majority of rural people in the United States actually live in metropolitan areas—these rural metropolitan people create "lots of conceptual confusion." Furthermore, the administrative boundaries that define rural and urban places change over time; this can create significant problems in longitudinal research. Researchers need to consider, said Lichter, how to define and categorize rural areas, including whether to divide and count by rural region, commuting zone, or rural neighborhood.

Lichter closed by saying that the current preoccupation with urban neighborhoods "has distracted attention from the larger question of how different dimensions of the residential context, which operate at multiple geographic and social scales, become salient in the lives of individuals and families." It is critical, he said, to break down the rural-urban divide and consider the multiple aspects and factors that impact individual's environment and outcomes.

DISCUSSION

Following the presentations, Mario Luis Small (Columbia University) led a discussion with speakers and workshop participants.

Current Trends

Small's first question was directed at Lichter. He noted that understanding the great migration during the 20th century is pivotal to understanding today's rural South and the urban East and Midwest. He asked Lichter to talk about the current trends in rural and urban areas that will improve understanding of what is happening in the 21st century. Lichter responded that there are several important things impacting the flow of people across the country. First, policy decisions that impact immigration and ports of entry can affect where people settle; for example, there has been a great migration to the Midwest for workers in meat packing, dairy farms, and hospitality. Second, the cost of living in many metropolitan areas is turning rural areas into a "collecting ground for America's poor." Both suburban and metropolitan people are moving in increasing proportions into rural areas because of lower cost of living and housing, he said. Furthermore, people who do have resources are moving into rural areas for second homes or retirement. This results in a process of rural gentrification, as the movement of urban people into an area makes it more difficult for the original rural population to stay.

Challenges for Rural Research

A second question for Lichter involved the challenges involved in studying rural areas. Small noted that researchers working in isolated, resource-deprived communities need a lot of "fortitude and commitment," particularly for longer-term ethnographic work. He asked Lichter to discuss potential ways to improve the quality of the data collected in rural areas, whether ethnographic, survey, or other types of data. Lichter responded that while there has been a lot of leadership in this area from the university community, one major challenge is that today's students and researchers largely have "no experience, no connection to rural America whatsoever." This lack of first-hand experience makes it difficult for researchers to gain entrée into some rural communities. For example, said Lichter, there are very, very few sociologists or economists who have spent time in the Delta, the colonias along the Rio Grande valley, or on American Indian reservations. "These are places you don't go if you're not on your way to anywhere else; they are forgotten places," he said.

Limitations of Tax Data

Small asked Staiger to comment on the limitations of using tax data to study mobility, as the Opportunity Atlas does. Small noted that research has found that tax records at the bottom of the distribution may not accurately reflect reality; since these are the populations "we most care about," how appropriate are these data to use? Staiger responded that while using tax data has many strengths, it is not a flawless approach. One way to make progress in both understanding the limitations to the data and taking steps to improve the data, he said, is to link tax data with other data sources. For example, tax data could be linked with Census data in order to determine to what extent tax data are missing some low-income families who do not file taxes. "When you collect data on an individual from multiple data sources, you can triangulate to determine a more accurate measure, as well as the strengths and weaknesses of different data sources," he said.

Private Data

A workshop participant asked Staiger about the potential role for leveraging cell phone GPS data or other private data to understand processes related to mobility. Staiger responded that there is "enormous potential" in the data owned by private companies, particularly in terms of understanding the role of neighborhoods in shaping economic mobility. For example, one strength is the large sample size that could allow researchers to create very local measures of characteristics of places. In addition, data such as those from Google or Facebook can be used to measure things that can typically not be captured in Census surveys or administrative records. Staiger gave one example of a way that cell phone data specifically could be used; he said that they could be used to track where people are moving in order to measure the extent to which roads and other neighborhood features are isolating communities from one another.

Looking Prospectively

Mobility research is valuable for explaining how policies and trends in the past have resulted in inequalities today, said Small. However, looking prospectively is more challenging. He asked Sharkey to opine on what current trends will end up being meaningful for the mobility of today's youth. "It is a mistake to predict the future," responded Sharkey. However, he said, intermediate outcomes can improve understanding of what is changing and how these changes might impact mobility. For example, research has focused on making precise causal estimates about how exposure to violence affects the economic outcomes of a young person. When violence levels change (such as the rise in crime in 2020), these estimates can be used to think about how the change might impact youth's prospects for mobility. Interventions could then be developed based on the inference that the rise in crime will have long-term effects. These interventions, he said, could be targeted directly at youth and families, or at the environment that will also be impacted by the rise in violence (e.g., businesses, schools).

Family and Spatial Processes

Another workshop participant observed a potential relationship between family processes and spatial disadvantage in mobility. She said that most individuals live near parents and adult children, but that this spatial clustering is more common among individuals who are disadvantaged. Thus, she said, the characteristics associated with lack of mobility are likely to be shared among these family members (e.g., local labor markets). Small asked Sharkey to comment on how family processes and spatial processes may intersect and reinforce one another. Sharkey agreed that there are mechanisms that can contribute to families sharing networks that can support people during difficult times and on which they can rely to stay in school or purchase a house, and so on. However, he said, there is a broader shift of rising inequality across regions, and the chances for upward mobility are now based on where a person spends the early part of their life. The implication, he said, is that variation across regions is much more important than it was a generation ago. Sharkey said that individuals from lower-mobility areas "have to balance the advantages and the supports that come from having networks rooted in a place" with the benefits that arise from moving to places that are economically more dynamic, with rising opportunities and wages. At this moment, he said, the "balance is tilted toward the benefits of making long-distance moves to areas of opportunity."

Why Do Neighborhoods Matter?

Although many speakers made the point that neighborhoods matter, said Small, he asked them to elaborate on *why* neighborhoods matter—what are the specific mechanisms that create advantage or disadvantage in mobility? Sharkey listed a number of neighborhood factors related to mobility, including violence, pollutants in water and air, and exposure to lead. However, instead of considering these factors on their own as mechanisms that lead to economic outcomes, Sharkey said he is trying to push toward a model that considers how neighborhoods relate to other neighborhoods in the community; for example, how policies and choices impact a poor neighborhood, a gated neighborhood, a neighborhood zoned for single-family residence, or a neighborhood with a highway surrounding it. Sharkey suggested that if someone doesn't think that neighborhoods matter, they should "immediately move to the most disadvantaged, most violent community" they can find because this move should not affect their lives in a negative way and will save them a great deal of money. This tongue-in-cheek suggestion, he said, makes the point that people have a natural intuition that dimensions of one's environment affect their later life outcomes.

The fact that neighborhoods matter is well established, said Staiger. For example, research shows that children who move to higher-opportunity neighborhoods at younger ages earn more in adulthood than children who move at older ages. While some mechanisms are established, there is ongoing, extensive research into the other mechanisms that lead to this relationship. For example, said Staiger, researchers are looking into richer measures that may impact mobility, such as social networks or friendships across class lines.

Small qualified his opening question by noting that while it is important to think about and be able to explain why neighborhoods matter, there has been a long history of work in this area. He shared two review papers[6,7]

---

[6] Sharkey, P., and Faber, J.W. 2014. Where, when, why, and for whom do residential contexts matter? Moving away from the dichotomous understanding of neighborhood effects. *Annual Review of Sociology*, 40(1), 559-579.
[7] Small, M., and Newman, K. 2001. Urban poverty after the truly disadvantaged: The rediscovery of the family, the neighborhood, and culture. *Annual Review of Sociology*, 27, 23-45.

that discuss this work, and noted that it is important to keep the long-term evidentiary basis in mind as new data are collected.

Depopulation

Recalling Lichter's comments about the "3 Ds," Small asked Lichter to comment further on the specific reasons why depopulation has an impact on mobility. Lichter responded that there is chronic outmigration of younger people from rural areas due to a lack of job opportunities. Often, he said, this is because the single industry in a town (e.g., timber, manufacturing) shuts down, so younger people move to find new opportunities. This leaves older people aging in place who are reluctant to spend money on schools or other youth-centered organizations. In addition, depopulation leads to community institutions, such as hospitals and supermarkets, closing down, furthering the existing disadvantages. However, Lichter noted, it is difficult to speak broadly about all rural communities; there are significant differences in the history, discrimination and oppression issues, and isolation among rural communities that range from American Indian reservations to Appalachia.

Data for Relational Studies

A workshop participant asked Sharkey to elaborate on what type of data are needed to measure and understand the relational aspects of neighborhoods, particularly contemporaneously. Sharkey responded by giving an example of his current research and explaining what kind of data are used. He and his colleagues have been working to build a dataset to examine how space is divided and how outcomes differ across these boundaries. They use data that includes information on city and town boundaries, school districts, gated communities, land zoning, and other public and private data. They have used these data to examine the issue of police violence by looking at the resources of local police departments across urban area commuting zones. Sharkey explained that communities with few resources and high levels of violence may struggle more with police violence than neighborhoods with a higher property tax base and more resources. This is one example, he said, of how data can be pulled together to document how inequality lays out across space and to identify the boundaries that form the spatial structure of inequality.

Major Approaches for Research

Small asked each speaker to briefly identify approaches for improving and expanding the type of research that is most needed in this area. Responses included:

- Rural research needs to be mainstreamed in the university. (Lichter)
- More resources need to be allocated to build datasets that allow researchers to drill into large data sets to observe how interventions impact people differently in different areas of the country. (Staiger)
- Students need rigorous training in areas including big data, data science, and ethnographic research. (Sharkey)

5

Studying Mobility by Race, Ethnicity, and Immigration Status

This session featured presentations and discussion about studying the influence of race, ethnicity, and immigration status on mobility. The first presentation provided a broad perspective on the challenges and opportunities for studying mobility by race. The second presentation examined how researchers can measure concepts such as structural racism and institutional discrimination, and identified research challenges and opportunities in this area. The third presentation considered immigration status and mobility, while the fourth focused on the diversity of the Asian American population.

Key Points Highlighted by the Presenters:

- Structural and systemic factors—such as structural racism—influence the rigidity of the economic system and thus the ability of an individual to experience upward mobility. (William "Sandy" Darity)
- Research is needed to develop and refine ways of measuring structural racism as a factor in mobility. (Tyson Brown)
- Studying immigration and mobility is more important than ever because the "new third generation" has arrived; these grandchildren of post-1965 immigrants can provide valuable insight into the status of immigrants and how they are doing compared with their parents and grandparents. (Tomás Jiménez)
- Data equity and disaggregation are critical to both understanding and serving the Asian American population; means and medians mask diverse outcomes, reify tropes, and result in exclusion from research and policy. (Jennifer Lee)

STUDYING MOBILITY BY RACE AND CLASS

Mobility can be upward or downward, said William ("Sandy") Darity (Duke University). There is a general consensus that good societies have a high degree of upward mobility. However, he said, an alternative view is that a good society is one in which a floor is set for well-being; that is, there is a point below which no one can fall. In the current U.S. system, there is no boundary to downward mobility; however, there is some degree of rigidity in upward mobility. The rigidity of a system, said Darity, is predicated on the boundaries on upward mobility, which in turn rely on the extent of structural stratification in the economic system. In order to understand this system of mobility, it is critical to understand and be able to measure the conditions that determine the degree of rigidity, for example, structural racism. There are efforts underway to measure structural racism, he said, but there are some serious conceptual issues. One of the central difficulties is "bouncing between" attempting to measure an outcome of structural racism and a component of structural racism.

Studying social mobility by race and class, said Darity, can mean looking at how social groups fare over the life course, or what happens intergenerationally for these groups. The term *social class*, he continued, is nebulous and can be defined a number of ways. It is conventionally defined by sociologists with a combination of occupation and income to create groups of bottom, working, middle, and upper classes. Alternatively, social class can be defined by educational attainment and asset ownership. Darity commented that he prefers a definition based solely on occupation, in which the "working class" are those engaged in productive labor, that is, who are neither business owners nor hired managers. Similarly, mobility can be measured in different ways, including by wealth or income. Darity has become "increasingly convinced" that wealth is a more compelling standard to assess individual or group opportunity and economic security.

Based on the definitions of social class and the use of wealth as a measurement of mobility, Darity shared his recent research on recovery after the 2007-2009 Great Recession.[1] In this research, Darity and his colleague examined intragroup mobility patterns over the course of the recession and its immediate aftermath. Darity shared three key findings

---

[1] Addo, F.R., and Darity, W.A. 2021. Disparate recoveries: Wealth, race, and the working class after the Great Recession. *The ANNALS of the American Academy of Political and Social Science*, 695(1), 173-192.

with workshop participants. First, during the recession, Black and Latino[2] households lost 48 percent and 44 percent of their wealth, respectively, while White households lost 26 percent. Second, whether professional or working class, Black- and Latino-led households were less likely than White households to reach the three upper wealth quintiles ("middle class" status or above). Third, the proportion of wealth-poor families generally decreased between 2010 and 2019, but it increased among Black professionals.

What is particularly noteworthy, said Darity, is the fact that the White working class has a net worth that significantly exceeds the net worth of professional class families who are Black or Latinx. He shared a graph that illustrates this "striking" disparity (see Figure 5-1). It is often asked, he said, why White working class people do not join with oppressed minorities in order to transform American society. This graph, he said, provides "very strong evidence as to why that doesn't typically occur"—the White working class is in a dramatically advantaged position relative to all other class groups of other races.

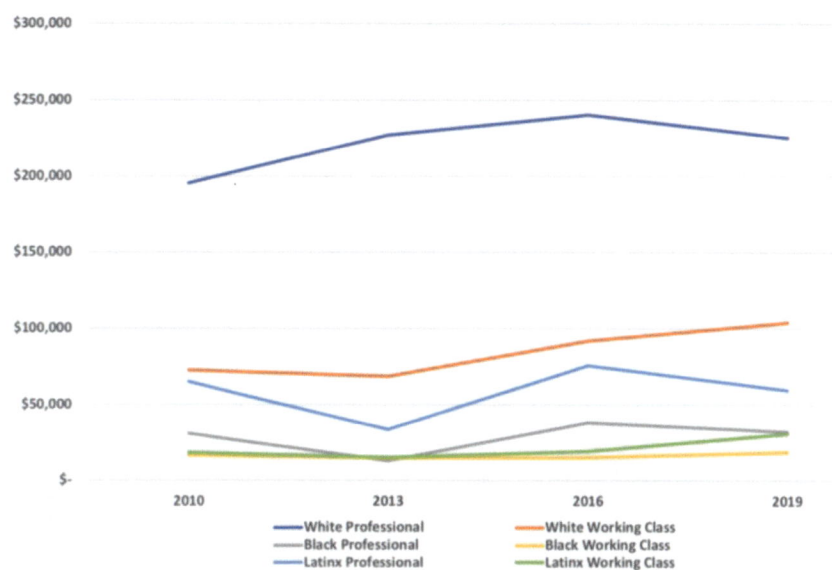

FIGURE 5-1 Median wealth among working class and professional class households.
SOURCE: Workshop presentation by William "Sandy" Darity, February 15, 2022.

---

[2] Usage of the terms *Latino*, *Latinx*, and *Hispanic* in the workshop proceedings reflects use by individual speakers.

MEASURES OF STRUCTURAL RACISM AND INSTITUTIONAL DISCRIMINATION

When it comes to mobility, said Tyson Brown (Duke University), place matters, and place is closely intertwined with race, racism, and opportunity structures. However, he said, understanding of these processes has been hindered by both conceptual and methodological gaps in the literature. Brown shared a figure (see Figure 5-2) that shows the evolution of the field of research on social mobility and race. Descriptive studies yield important information about racial differences in social mobility patterns, he said, and the field has largely moved beyond discredited biological and cultural deficit explanations. Research has also demonstrated the limited utility of behavioral economic and human capital explanations for racial inequities. Some researchers suggest that residual disparities that exist after accounting for behaviors are attributed to discrimination. However, these approaches operate under the "untenable assumption" that racism does not shape economic decisions and the acquisition of human capital in the first place. With this evolution in understanding, it is becoming clear that focusing solely on individual factors leads to an incomplete and biased understanding of the drivers of racial inequities and social mobility.

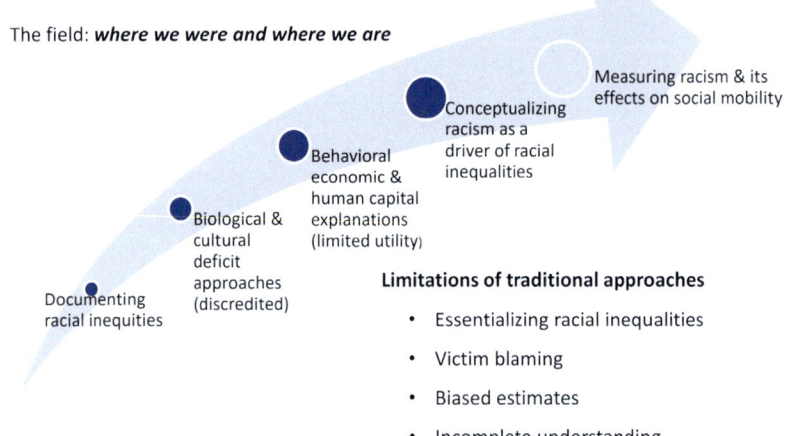

FIGURE 5-2 Evolution of the field of social mobility and race.
SOURCE: Workshop presentation by Tyson Brown, February 15, 2022.

Researchers have increasingly moved toward a conceptualization of racial inequities in social mobility as a consequence of structural racism, said Brown. However, relatively few studies have empirically tested this proposition; skeptics point to the dearth of quantitative research on the topic, and dismiss structural racism as a slippery concept for which robust empirical evidence is lacking. As a field, said Brown, there is an opportunity to gain empirical traction by measuring structural racism and its effects on social mobility. This will enable researchers to answer new and salient questions, to use more rigorous research designs, and to build a knowledge base to inform more efficacious racial equity solutions.

In order to move forward toward this potential, Brown offered several research priorities for the field. First, researchers should utilize core tenets of structural theories to guide measurement approaches. Second, there is a need to develop novel, theory-informed, multi-sectoral measures of structural racism. Third, mapping structural racism can build a better understanding of the geographic variation in racial exclusion and subordination. Fourth, the impact of structural racism on mobility patterns should be estimated by linking contextual structural racism measures with geocoded data on mobility. Finally, he said, building a publicly available data infrastructure on structural racism could lower barriers to this type of research and catalyze research on differential mobility processes. Brown focused the remainder of his presentation on the first three research priorities.

Utilizing Core Tenets

There are a number of challenges to measuring structural racism, said Brown, because it is a "complex and insidious de facto phenomena" that is often hidden and not directly observed in modern society. It is therefore unsurprising, he said, that there are relatively few empirical studies that explicitly measure the impact of structural racism on social mobility. However, there are several theoretical frameworks that offer foundational grounding for understanding how dimensions of structural racism intersect and work together as a system. Brown shared a study in which he and his colleague scoped the broader literature in order to identify central tenets of structural racism theories.[3] They distilled these foundational ideas into a definition that provides conceptual and analytical clarity: "structural racism involves a multifaceted, interconnected, and institutionalized system of racial insubordination for people of color, and superordination for Whites, and this is observable in manifest concrete racial inequalities in life out-

---

[3] Brown, T., and Homan, P. 2022, March 21. Structural racism and health stratification in the U.S.: Connecting theory to measurement. *SocArcXiv.* https://doi.org/10.31235/osf.io/3eacp

comes." In short, said Brown, structural racism refers to the systemic, racial exclusion from power, resources, opportunities, and well-being.

Structural racism is embedded in political, economic, medical, criminal, legal, and social institutions, and is observable as racial inequities in outcomes in education, occupation, wealth, health, political representation, incarceration, and housing. Structural racism can be considered a fundamental factor that drives racialized disadvantages, because it shapes access to both immediate economic resources and opportunities, as well as exposure to social and economic risk. Because of its multifaceted, interconnected, and institutionalized nature, it is likely that structural racism impacts mobility through many different intervening mechanisms, he said.

Developing Measures

Empirical studies on structural racism are often out of step with theoretical insights, said Brown, and they have a number of limitations. For example, studies have typically relied on single indicators of structural racism, which are useful but often subject to measurement error. Alternatively, they have examined several indicators, but done so separately, thereby overlooking relationships among structural forms of racism and how they operate as a system to shape life outcomes. These approaches, said Brown, fail to capture the extent to which indicators of structural racism are interconnected and reflect an underlying latent construct, and they also lead to an incomplete understanding and biased estimates of the impact of structural racism on mobility. Furthermore, he said, much of the research on structural racism measurement has been focused at the meso-level, in particular the neighborhood and county levels. While these levels are important, the literature has largely ignored or overlooked more macro-level units, such as states. However, a few recent studies use administrative and publicly available data to examine state-level structural racism; these studies span domains including judicial, educational, economic, political, and segregation. Investigating structural racism at the state level is a "major advance," said Brown, yet few studies have examined the joint consequences of multi-sectoral structural racism. Brown shared details of his recent work that aims to measure structural racism in ways that align with structural theories. Brown and his colleague used nine indicators of structural racism to develop a latent measure of structural racism, using confirmatory factor analysis to measure the extent to which structural racism across domains is reflective of an underlying latent construct.[4] Brown conveyed his hope that these sorts of approaches to capturing and measuring structural racism will provide a proof of concept to "get empirical traction on the drivers of racial inequalities."

---

[4] Ibid.

Mapping Structural Racism

Theory and evidence both suggest that the manifestations, as well as the modalities, of structural racism vary spatially. For example, Figure 5-3 maps structural racism across states, using the structural racism latent scale Brown and his colleague developed. The patterns in this map are consistent with the idea that states, which operate as political, social, cultural, legal, and administrative units, vary in their degree of structural racism and function as institutional actors contributing to the unequal distribution of resources. Brown noted that recent events, including the pandemic, have "laid bare" the role of states in shaping inequality in general and racial inequality in particular.

To test the utility of the latent measure of structural racism, Brown and his colleague linked it to geocoded health and demographic survey data. The results revealed that state-level structural racism is predictive of an array of health outcomes; specifically, exposure to higher levels of structural racism at the state level is associated with worse health outcomes for Black people, but not White people.[5] There is a growing body of research on developing novel measures of structural racism in the population health literature, said Brown. For example, a recent study[6] conducted a latent class analysis on structural racism at the county level, spanning several domains, including segregation, home ownership, education, employment, and in-

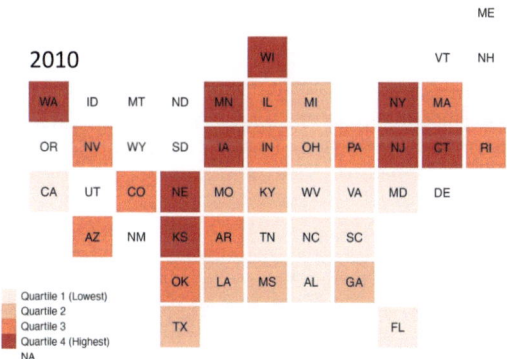

FIGURE 5-3 Geography of structural racism by state.
NOTE: NA = not assessed.
SOURCE: Workshop presentation by Tyson Brown, February 15, 2022.

---

[5] Ibid.
[6] Hardeman, R.R., Homan, P.A., Chantarat, T., Davis, B.A., and Brown, T.H. 2022. Improving the measurement of structural racism to achieve antiracist health policy. *Health Affairs (Millwood), 41*(2),179-186.

come; the study found that structural racism in these areas is predictive of health outcomes. Brown argued that this line of inquiry could be expanded by empirically testing the extent to which there are distinct typologies of structural racism, at multiple levels, and how they affect racialized mobility processes. This would be an "innovative direction for the field."

It is also important, he said, to directly measure how social mobility is affected by policy contexts. A 2021 project[7] developed a publicly available database of laws related to structural racism. Another project looked at how state-level immigration policies may impact health outcomes for Latinx people.[8] One question that can be examined by mapping existing data sources is the extent to which social mobility is impacted by cultural and ideological forms of anti-Blackness. While some measures such as racial animus and racial biases are established, there is an opportunity to utilize innovative data and methods to capture new aspects of anti-Blackness. For example, geocoded data from internet search engines can be used to capture racial animus in a state's population.

Mapping historical racism can help illuminate how history directs, constructs, and molds contemporary structural racism. In that vein, said Brown, several empirical studies[9] have found that regions that had larger enslaved proportions of population in 1860 have greater present-day inequalities in poverty and economic mobility, as well as higher levels of pro-White bias. Other findings of these studies include that historical redlining practices underlie contemporary residential segregation patterns, and that New Deal policies expanded the White middle class and are "directly implicated" in modern racial inequalities in wealth. Further research, said Brown, should explicitly test the extent to which contemporary social mobility is affected by historical racism—for example, how variations in exposure to slavery, Jim Crow laws, or racialized voter suppression impact mobility.

---

[7] Agénor, M., Perkins, C., Stamoulis, C., Hall, R.D., Samnaliev, M., Berland, S., and Bryn, A.S. 2021. Developing a database of structural racism-related state laws for health equity research and practice in the United States. *Public Health Reports,* 136(4),428-440.

[8] Philbin, M.M., Flake, M., Hatzenbuehler, M.L., and Hirsch, J.S. 2018. State-level immigration and immigrant-focused policies as drivers of Latino health disparities in the United States. *Social Science and Medicine,* 199, 29-38.

[9] Bloome, D., and Muller, C. 2015. Tenancy and African American marriage in the postbellum South. *Demography,* 52(5), 1409-1430; Darity, W., and Mullen, A.K. 2020. *From Here to Equality: Reparations for Black Americans in the Twenty-First Century.* Chapel Hill: University of North Carolina Press. Williams, J.A., Logan, T.D., and Hardy, B.L. 2021. The persistence of historical racial violence and political suppression: Implications for contemporary regional inequality. *The ANNALS of the American Academy of Political and Social Science,* 694(1), 92-107. Muller, C. and Wildeman, C. 2016. Geographic variation in the cumulative risk of imprisonment and parental imprisonment in the United States. *Demography,* 53(5), 1499-1509.

Brown shared an example of a research project[10] that used a structural intersectionality approach to population health; researchers examined the relationships between macro-level structural racism, structural sexism, and economic inequality, and linked these data to state-level measures of individual health. Their analysis, he said, showed that structural forms of justice intersect in a variety of ways, but do not strongly covary across states. Furthermore, they found that the joint effects of structural oppression were most deleterious to Black women, followed by Black men and White women. White men's health, said Brown, was "largely unaffected" by intersecting forms of structural oppression. This study could serve as a springboard and potential data source for similar studies aimed at understanding how intersectional oppressions shape mobility.

STUDYING MOBILITY BY IMMIGRATION STATUS

Studying mobility among immigrant populations continues to have relevance, said Tomás Jiménez (Stanford University), as one-quarter of today's population is either a first- or second-generation immigrant. The framework for this research goes back to the origins of the study of immigrant groups in the United States, he said, introducing workshop participants to the definition of the word *generation* as it is used by immigration scholars. First generation refers to immigrants themselves; their children are referred to as second generation and grandchildren third. This conceptualization of generation is based on assimilation theories that sought to explain the experiences of late-19th- and early-20th-century southern and eastern European immigrants. This theory holds that there is change between immigrant generations across time; each new generation born in the United States tends to have more education and more income, be less residentially segregated and more likely to intermarry, and their ethnic identity becomes less important over time.

Jiménez described how immigration patterns have changed over the years. First, starting in 1965, immigrants largely come from non-European origins; most are from Latin America with a sizable proportion from Asia (see Figure 5-4). Second, there is a large undocumented population among today's immigrants. The size of the undocumented population peaked shortly before the 2007-2009 Great Recession, declined precipitously and has remained relatively flat. One misconception about the population of undocumented immigrants, he said, is that they are newcomers to the country. In reality, about two-thirds of undocumented immigrants have lived in the

---

[10] Homan, P., Brown, T.H., and King, B. 2021. Structural intersectionality as a new direction for health disparities research. *Journal of Health and Social Behavior*, 62(3), 350-370. https://doi.org/10.1177/00221465211032947

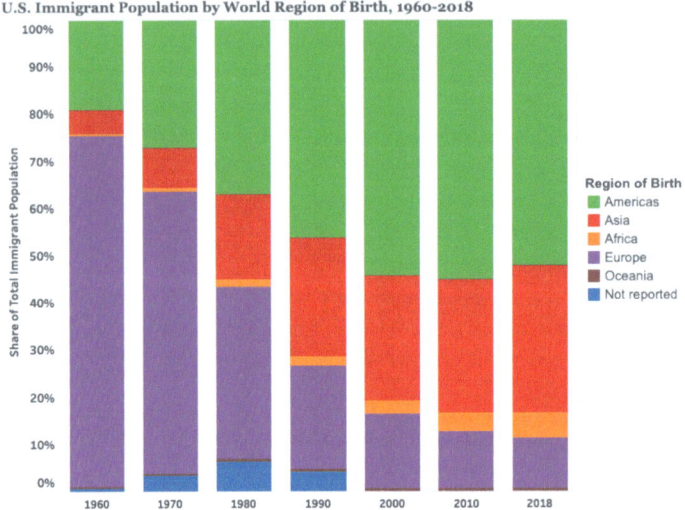

FIGURE 5-4 Regions of birth for immigrants in the United States, 1960-2018.
SOURCE: Workshop presentation by Tomás Jiménez, February 15, 2022.

United States for more than 10 years. This fact has significant implications for understanding mobility, said Jiménez. The third important characteristic about today's immigrant population is that immigrants are distributed across the country "in ways that we have never seen before." There are still significant concentrations of immigrants in California, the eastern corridor, the southern part of Florida, and the U.S.-Mexico border, but there are now new areas of concentration in the Midwest and the South.

In spite of these changes, the approach for studying mobility among immigrant populations still involves a close examination of the differences between immigrant generations, said Jiménez. The typical way of doing this is comparing all first-generation immigrants to all second-generation immigrants and so on. Jiménez, in contrast, advocates for a model that takes into account not just the immigrant generations, but also the time period that these immigrant generations come from. He shared a figure from a 2008 book[11] that illustrates this model (see Figure 5-5).

There are several challenges involved in studying immigrants and mobility, said Jiménez. There is a lack of large government or non-government surveys that track immigrant generations. The Current Population Survey is an exception because it asks whether people and their parents were

---

[11] Telles, E., and Ortiz, V. 2008. *Generations of Exclusion: Mexican Americans, Assimilation, and Race*. New York: Russell Sage Foundation.

STUDYING MOBILITY BY RACE, ETHNICITY, AND IMMIGRATION STATUS 61

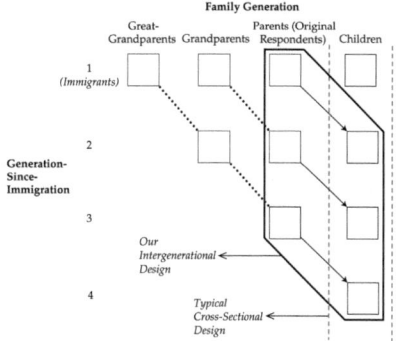

FIGURE 5-5 Two dimensions of generational change.
SOURCE: Telles, E., and Ortiz, V. 2008. *Generations of Exclusion: Mexican Americans, Assimilation, and Race*. New York: Russel Sage Foundation.

born in the United States; however, it still remains difficult to track the third generation and higher. For example, if a respondent said that they and their parents were born in the United States, they could be post-1965 third-generation immigrants, or they could be fifth-generation descendants of immigrants who arrived more than 100 years ago. This difference is very important in a society "where we have experienced tremendous demographic, social, political, and economic change because of the recent arrival of immigrants." In the 1990s, social scientists made particular effort to understand the children of immigrants, said Jiménez, but there has been no similar effort to understand the grandchildren of immigrants.

There are also intellectual challenges in immigration studies, he said, such as the common distinction that is made between race and immigration scholarship. Jiménez argued that this is a false distinction, and that "one cannot begin to understand race in the United States today and mobility without understanding differences in immigrant generations, and one cannot begin to understand differences in immigrant generations without understanding race." Another challenge is an increasing tendency to homogenize ethnoracial groups and to treat them as if they are "hermetically sealed units" that do not change internally. Instead, he said, these groups should be seen as dynamic and internally differentiated, and research should focus not just on mean outcomes of an ethnoracial group but on the distribution of differences within the group as well. The third challenge in this area, he said, is that the ideas of assimilation, integration, and incorporation are "unfashionable"; he argued, however, that they remain essential to the study of immigrants in the United States.

Studying immigration and mobility is more important than ever, said Jiménez, because the "new third generation" has arrived. These grandchildren of post-1965 immigrants can give great insight into the status of immigrants and how they are doing compared to their parents and grandparents. Jiménez shared details from his work in this area[12]; the study compared second generation immigrants from 1980 to third-generation immigrants from 2010. Jiménez and his colleagues looked at measures such as family structure, educational attainment, household income, and poverty status. This study was in part a "proof of concept" project to show the importance of studying this new third generation because they are the generation in which there is often a huge shift in mobility outcomes. Jiménez closed by advocating for a concerted effort to track down the actual second-generation immigrants who were studied in the 1990s and their third-generation children; this would allow researchers to track changes between individuals and their parents and grandparents without constructing synthetic cohorts.

MOBILITY AMONG ASIAN AMERICANS

Asian Americans are one of the fastest-growing populations in the United States, said Jennifer Lee (Columbia University); the percentage of Asian Americans in the United States nearly doubled between 2000 and 2020, and is expected to double again by 2060. Unlike some other ethnoracial groups, the population of Asian Americans is growing primarily through immigration, and by 2055, Asian Americans will surpass Hispanic Americans as the largest immigrant group in the country. Two out of three Asian Americans are first-generation immigrants and 90 percent are either immigrants or the children of immigrants. Moreover, said Lee, one in seven Asian immigrants is undocumented, and this population is growing at a faster pace than the population of undocumented immigrants from Mexico or Central America. Asian Americans are a diverse group, coming from countries including China, Korea, the Philippines, India, Pakistan, and Cambodia. Lee noted that this heterogeneity is often not acknowledged in the United States, which leads to biased assumptions about Asian Americans' opportunities and outcomes. At one end of the distribution are highly educated, hyper-selected Asian immigrants from areas such as Taiwan and India, and at the other end are Southeast Asian refugees from countries such as Bhutan and Laos.

This diversity, said Lee, is often obscured by means and medians; she emphasized the importance of disaggregating data in order to understand, serve, and protect the rights of the Asian American population. For example, a detailed count of the Asian population is essential to providing

---

[12] Jiménez, T.R., Park, J., and Pedroza, J. 2018. The new third generation: Post-1965 immigration and the next chapter in the long story of assimilation. *International Migration Review*, 52(4), 1040-1079.

voting materials in appropriate languages. Furthermore, she added, Asian Americans are the group most likely to be concerned that answers they provide on the Census will be used against them. This institutional distrust also affects Asian Americans' willingness to report hate crimes and violence, which surged during the COVID-19 pandemic. "When we consider opportunities and challenges related to inclusion and mobility among Asian Americans," said Lee, "building institutional trust must be part of the conversation." Unfortunately, said Lee, there is a "glaring lack" of investment in Asian American communities, from both the federal government and private foundations. For example, the National Institutes of Health invested only 0.17 percent of its budget between 1992 and 2018 in Asian American communities,[13] and foundations awarded only 0.20 percent in 2018 to this community.[14]

Lee closed with several recommendations for improving research, and ultimately outcomes, for the Asian American population. First, collection categories should be expanded for Asian subpopulations, Native Hawaiian and Pacific Islander subpopulations, and gender identity. Second, researchers should adopt the American Community Survey practice of collecting information on country of birth of both the respondent and the parent. Lee's third recommendation was to seek data equity in all stages of research design, analysis, and dissemination. For example, data collection instruments should be linguistically and culturally appropriate in order to serve a population in which two-thirds are immigrants and one-third is limited in English language proficiency. Fourth, Lee emphasized the importance of building institutional trust among Asian Americans; this involves including community leaders and scientific experts at all stages of data collection, as well as creating scientific advisory committees and community advisory committees. Finally, Lee called for more investment in the Asian American population. She noted that after the surge in anti-Asian violence during the COVID-19 pandemic, there has been "unprecedented interest and surge in investment." This is an opportunity to "break from the past" and to include Asian Americans in research and investment.

---

[13] Đoàn, L.N., Takata, Y., Sakuma, K., and Irvin, V.L. 2019. Trends in clinical research including Asian American, Native Hawaiian, and Pacific Islander participants funded by the US National Institutes of Health, 1992 to 2018. *JAMA Network Open*, 2(7), e197432. https://doi.org/10.1001/jamanetworkopen.2019.7432

[14] Asian Americans/Pacific Islanders in Philanthropy (AAPIP). 2021. *Seeking to Soar: Foundation Funding for Asian American and Pacific Islander Communities.* https://aapip.org/resources/seeking-to-soar-foundation-funding-for-asian-american-and-pacific-islander-communities

DISCUSSION

Following the presentations, Trevon Logan (The Ohio State University) and Kathleen Mullan Harris (University of North Carolina at Chapel Hill) moderated a discussion with speakers and workshop participants.

The Concept of Race

Logan began the discussion session by noting that while presenters talked at length about definitions of structural racism and racial inequities, there was no discussion of "what race is in and of itself." Logan argued that in this context, race should be defined as a political variable, because it influences the distribution of resources and has an inherent dimension of power. He asked speakers to comment on whether using a political definition of race would alter the study of mobility, and whether it could open up new avenues to think about solutions to inequities. Darity responded that he personally views race as a political construct because it is an instrument "for the purposes of giving one social group an advantage over others, and to rationalize that advantage." However, Darity said he was not sure that thinking of race as political rather than a social variable would change research or analysis; researchers generally rely on self-reported race, which is a construct that emerges out of social experiences. Brown agreed with Logan that race is a historical and political construct, rather than merely a demographic characteristic. Race was made through a political process, and it is dynamic, fluid, and "highly contested." Brown said that this does have implications for research, and that there is an opportunity to rethink how to collect and interpret self-report measures of race by taking a more contextual approach. Darity added that this historical and political approach to race can be examined through the lens of stratification economics, which looks at how relative group position plays a role in the behavior of individuals and social groups. Brown agreed and said new data and tools are available for mapping aspects of historical oppression and violence in order to better understand patterns and drivers of inequality and mobility.

Mobility in Immigrant Populations

Harris asked Lee and Jiménez to elaborate on what past mobility research in immigrant populations has shown, and where the research should go moving forward. Jiménez responded that the patterns of mobility for immigrants today look similar to the patterns of 100 years ago, and for some measures, upward mobility is happening faster. For example, he said, intermarriage rates among second-generation immigrants are high, with about 30 percent of third-generation Hispanic American children growing up with one Hispanic parent and one non-Hispanic parent. Intermarriage is a "key measure of integration," said Jiménez. When looking at the research, said Lee, it is important to keep in mind the difference between mobility and outcomes. For example, second-generation Chinese Americans have high educational attainment, but the rate does not vary significantly from their first-generation parents. On the other hand, second-generation Mexican Americans have much higher educational attainment than their parents, being two to three times as likely to graduate from college. When considering "success" among immigrant populations, the conversation is often focused on outcomes rather than mobility, she said. Another interesting pattern, said Lee, is that women in the immigrant community are more likely to graduate from college than men, particularly in the more disadvantaged groups.

Jiménez added that an undocumented status can have a large effect on mobility, even for future generations who are born in the United States. Research has found that for immigrants who were able to legalize, their children's and grandchildren's outcomes were "far and away" better than the outcomes of descendants of immigrants who could not legalize. Undocumented status is a "penalty" to the classic mobility outcomes, he said.

Structural Measures in Immigration

Noting that Darity and Brown discussed the importance of structural factors in studying race and mobility, Harris asked Lee and Jiménez what types of structural measures are important in the immigration space. Jiménez said that immigration scholars have been calling for large government surveys to ask for parent place of birth, and ideally grandparent place of birth as well. He acknowledged that if surveys included all of the questions that social scientists wanted, they would be inappropriately lengthy, but emphasized the importance of capturing this information in order to understand the generational shifts that are occurring. If large government surveys do not do this work, he said, there needs to be investment in nongovernmental efforts. Lee told workshop participants about her work with the STAATUS (Social Tracking of Asian Americans in the United States) index, and its questions about perceptions of Asian Americans. For example, the survey asks questions about whether respondents think that Asian Americans are "at least partly responsible" for COVID-19. Surveys that focus on racial attitudes, said Lee, often ignore attitudes toward Asian Americans, and Asian Americans are often not included in conversations about race or immigration. It is imperative, said Lee, that future research looks at the experiences of this population as well as the attitudes toward them.

Mobility Over the Life Course

Previous speakers in the workshop discussed how measures of mobility—for example, income or wealth—often change significantly over the life course, said Harris. She asked speakers to comment on how the life course approach applies in the context of studying mobility and race and immigration. Darity responded that the wealth differential by race widens sharply as people age; it is at its smallest when people are in their 20s and 30s. If policies designed to close the wealth gap are based on data collected early in life, they can be "quite misleading." Darity suggested that measuring wealth at age 60 would be most appropriate, because it reflects the cumulative consequences of their life experiences. Furthermore, he said, the best predictor of an individual's eventual wealth position is the wealth position of their parents and grandparents. An individual's net worth is not generally a consequence of "careful and deliberate acts of personal savings," but instead is impacted by the advantages they receive from the previous generations. A final point, said Darity, is that educational attainment has a very weak relationship to reducing wealth disparities by race. For example, Black heads of household with a college degree have a lower median net worth than White heads of household who never finished high school. When it comes to wealth accumulation, he said, it is the intergenerational transmission mechanisms that are decisive. Brown added that this point is important when considering approaches for reducing racial inequality. Measuring wealth later in life is useful for capturing cumulative consequences, he said, but it is unclear where interventions would be most helpful. For example, should "baby bonds" be distributed when people reach the ages of 18 or 20, or would interventions at age 30 or 40 be more impactful? To answer these types of questions, said Brown, researchers need longitudinal data to capture all of the factors that matter to outcomes, and when they occur. He asked: are there "sensitive periods" that make a big difference, and when are these periods?. The next iteration of research in this area, he said, needs to go beyond the static snapshot to follow people in place and time, both within and between generations.

Darity gave his opinion on what policy would be appropriate for addressing racial wealth differences. He said that reparations for Black American descendants of slavery is the "only way to do it." The "baby bonds" proposal is directed at all Americans, so it would not have a powerful effect on the racial wealth gap.

When considering the life course perspective for immigrant populations, said Lee, there are two major factors that impact mobility. First, limited English language proficiency is a critical issue for some immigrant populations, and directing resources to this area is necessary to help them have the resources to be "a part of our society." Second, a pathway to citizenship is critical to inclusion, both for the first generation and for subsequent generations. Having a parent who was not able to naturalize significantly affects mobility outcomes for the second and third generations. Jiménez added that the understanding of the second generation is "stuck in late adolescence." He further stated that investing in research to understand where these individuals are now, and when they are in their 30s, 40s, and 50s, is "incredibly important."

Reparations

Following up on Darity's comment that reparations for Black American descendants of slavery are the only way to address racial wealth differences, a workshop participant asked how eligibility would be determined, given that many Americans have mixed ancestry or are descended from more recent immigrants. Darity said that he has long recommended two criteria for eligibility. First is a "lineage standard," in which an individual would have to demonstrate that they have at least one ancestor who was enslaved in the United States. The second criteria would require individuals to show that they self-identified as Black, Negro, African American, or Afro-American on a legal document at least 12 years before the adoption of a reparations plan. These criteria, he said, would eliminate the issue of White Americans who have an enslaved ancestor being eligible for reparations. To facilitate this process, Darity recommended that the federal government provide genealogical services to individuals seeking to make a claim.

Geography of Structural Racism

A workshop participant asked Brown to elaborate on the map of structural racism that he shared (see Figure 5-3), noting that some of the results were counter to what he expected to see, for example, that structural racism was higher in the Northeast than in the South. Brown responded that the structural racism measure includes factors that are particularly acute in Northeast and Midwestern states, such as inequalities in education, housing, political domains, employment, and criminal justice. While the reasons for these inequalities are not completely understood, scholars posit that the contemporary structural racism in the North has its roots in institutionalized policies and practices that were created in response to the Great Migration. These policies—such as redlining, racial covenants, and discriminatory policing—were codified because northern White populations perceived the incoming Black populations as a threat. There is a growing body of evidence, said Brown, that shows that Black/White inequalities are greatest in the Northeast and Midwest. However, he cautioned, this does not mean that individuals in these areas are doing worse than individuals in other areas; the South is "unique and pathogenic in all sorts of ways that are problematic." The greatest overall disadvantage is often found in the South, particularly in Appalachia. It is important, he said, to research and understand both absolute well-being and inequalities between groups.

Measures and Outcomes of Structural Racism

Harris asked Darity and Brown to comment on the need to distinguish between structural racism itself and its outcomes, which are often used as measures of structural racism. Specifically, she asked how they theorize about the causal mechanisms that link mesolevel indices with outcomes of interest. Brown responded that he thinks of the multifaceted scale of structural racism as reflecting a hidden or latent complex system. In this system, there are an array of pathways through which structural racism impacts outcomes, including health, economic capital, autonomy, power, and risk. For example, social stressors such as toxic living conditions and stigma are also drivers of inequality, he said. Brown argued for an approach in which structural racism is not measured by single indicators, but instead is considered as a system. This approach avoids certain types of measurement error and bias, he said, and also more realistically reflects the phenomena observed. Research in this area is still in its infancy, and there are opportunities to further explore specific causal pathways as well as the indirect effects of structural racism.

6

Data Infrastructure for Studying Mobility

As discussed by other speakers in the workshop, data are critical to studying mobility, and emerging sources of data can be leveraged to improve understanding. In this session, speakers discussed the use of administrative data and non-traditional data, as well as best practices for data governance.

Key Points Highlighted by the Presenters:

- Linking administrative data with survey data has the potential to drastically expand understanding of mobility in the United States. (Katie Genadek)
- Using educational data and neighborhood data to understand patterns of inequality can push interventions forward and provide intermediate-level outcomes to measure success. (Daniel Botting)
- Data on bank accounts and transactions can be used to better understand economic mobility, including how households are affected by shocks; the large sample size in banking data facilitates findings on subgroups. (Fiona Greig)
- Striking a balance between data access and data privacy is challenging but essential. (Katharine Abraham)

ADMINISTRATIVE DATA

There is a long history of studying mobility in the United States, said Katie Genadek (U.S. Census Bureau). She shared a series of articles from over the years that looked at mobility, including a 1962 paper that examined the proportion of men whose occupation was in the same occupation group as their fathers[1] and a 1974 paper on patterns of intergenerational mobility of females through marriage.[2] Mobility research, she said, is often driven in part by the availability of data. For example, occupational change has been used as a metric for mobility in part because historical data on occupation is widely available. Social and occupational mobility surveys (such as the General Social Survey) are a major source of data in this area, said Genadek, although they have limitations, including expense, small sample size, and limited geographic coverage. Administrative data, on the other hand, is already obtained, has wide geographic coverage, and may include relationship information. Genadek offered three examples of recent work relying on administrative data to study social mobility.[3]

The real opportunity, however, is in linking administrative data to survey data. Combining these two sources of data, said Genadek, adds demographic characteristics, socioeconomic variables, and detailed family information to administrative data, as well as additional outcomes of occupation, educational attainment, and housing. Genadek identified four recent examples of research that links administrative data with survey data.[4] Commonly used sources of administrative data include Social Security Administration records and tax records; commonly used sources of survey data include the Census, the American Community Survey, the Current Population Survey, and the Survey of Income and Program Participation.

Administrative records have both benefits and drawbacks, said Genadek. They generally have good coverage of the population, although it is more difficult to link individuals who are transient or who do not have a social security number. It is easiest to link taxpayers, workers, individuals

---

[1] https://www.census.gov/library/publications/1964/demo/p23-011.html
[2] Glenn, N.D., Ross, A.A., and Tully, J.C. 1974. Patterns of intergenerational mobility of females through marriage. *American Sociological Review*, 39, 683.
[3] Chetty, R., Hendren, N., Kline, P., and Saez, E. 2014. Where is the land of opportunity? The geography of intergenerational mobility in the United States. *The Quarterly Journal of Economics*, 129(4), 1553-1623; Mitnik, P., Bryant, V., Weber, M., and Grusky, D. 2015. *New Estimates of Intergenerational Mobility Using Administrative Data*. SOI Working Paper, Statistics of Income Division, Internal Revenue Service; Larrimore, J., Mortenson, J., and Splinter, D. 2015. *Income and Earnings Mobility in U.S. Tax Data* (July 30, 2015). FEDS Working Paper No. 2015-061, http://dx.doi.org/10.17016/FEDS.2015.061
[4] Mazumder, B. 2014. Black–White differences in intergenerational economic mobility in the United States. *Economic Perspectives*, 38(1). Akee, R., Jones, M.R., and Porter, S.R. 2019. Race matters: Income shares, income inequality, and income mobility for All U.S. Races. *Demography*, 56(3), 999-1021; Song, X., and Coleman, T. 2020. *Using Administrative Big Data to Solve Problems in Social Science and Policy Research*. University of Pennsylvania Population Center Working Paper (PSC/PARC), 2020-58; Chetty, R., Friedman, J., Hendren, N., and Stepner, M. 2020. *The Economic Impacts of COVID-19: Evidence from a New Public Database Built Using Private Sector Data*. NBER Working Paper No. 27431. Cambridge, MA: National Bureau of Economic Research.

on Medicare, individuals receiving government assistance, and men who have registered for the draft. Genadek shared a map that shows the percentage of population that can be linked to administrative records (see Figure 6-1); there are obvious gaps and areas where linkages are more difficult. Another challenge is that linkages with administrative data are generally only available for more recent generations; Genadek noted that there are also data before 1940, but there is a significant gap between 1950 and 2000. One solution to this issue is building out the U.S. Census Bureau's data linkage infrastructure; Genadek said she is currently working on this project. Another new resource is representative survey samples linked to lifetime Social Security Administration data.[5] These data have existed for years, but are now available to everyone, she said. Also available are large-scale U.S. Census linkages; Genadek noted that around 72 percent of young people in the 1940 Census can be linked forward to the 2000 Census. What was missing, however, are the data from the years 1950-1990. Capturing these data was challenging, she said, because the names are handwritten, the forms are stored on microfilm reels, and the data are highly restricted. Fortunately, researchers found that names could be efficiently recovered from these records, and they could be captured with sufficiently high quality to be linked into the existing systems. Now, a project is underway to use this approach to scan the microfilm reels with Census records from 1960 to

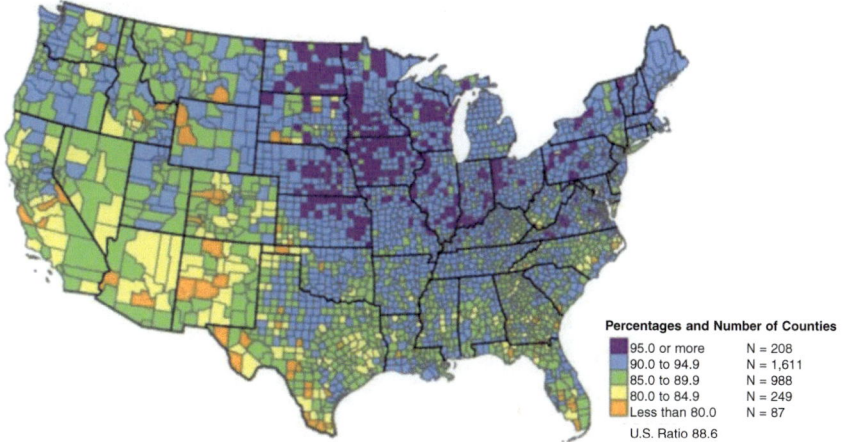

FIGURE 6-1 Proportion of population with available linked administrative data.
SOURCE: 2010 Census Match Study Report. https://www.census.gov/content/dam/Census/library/publications/2012/dec/2010_cpex_247.pdf

---

[5] Genadek, K.R., Hoyakem, C., and Pendergast, P.T. 2021. *The Summary Earning Record and Detailed Record Extracts*. Working Paper Number ADEP-WP-2021-15. https://www.census.gov/library/working-papers/2021/econ/earnings-record-extracts.html

1990, and to link the records to current data. Genadek said that the longitudinal infrastructure available in 2026 should include all linked decennial censuses, as well as surveys and administrative records. All of these data are available through the Federal Statistical Research Data Centers.

NONTRADITIONAL DATA SOURCES

School and Neighborhood Data

At this workshop, speakers have discussed the utility of educational data for examining social mobility, and how neighborhoods have a large impact on social mobility, said Daniel Botting (Impact Tulsa). Impact Tulsa, he said, is an organization committed to improving mobility for all students in the Tulsa region, with a focus on education. The network of public schools and nonprofits, businesses, and community leaders works on the "cradle-to-career" continuum from kindergarten to employment. Part of this work, said Botting, was using information from the Opportunity Atlas to examine the Tulsa community and to communicate with leaders about what is needed. While the Opportunity Atlas was a great starting point, he said, there was a need to better understand how neighborhood factors affect student outcomes in the current moment—not years later. Impact Tulsa created a tool called the Child Equity Index (CEI) in order to understand the social and environmental conditions that contribute to or hinder student opportunity, as well as to be able to identify and address schools and neighborhoods with higher needs. Botting said they wanted to move beyond "simply blaming schools" and move toward investing in community factors that matter.

The CEI uses data on a wide variety of student demographics, Botting explained, paired with neighborhood statistics on factors such as crime, unemployment rates, walkability, access to transit and grocery stores, land use, and life expectancy (see Figure 6-2). All of these data were used to build a model to estimate the impact of these factors on student academic outcomes, such as test scores and attendance. Botting expressed the hope of expanding the model in the future to look at data points such as graduation or college attendance.

When the CEI was created, said Botting, "we found exactly what we thought we would find." Neighborhoods matter for academic outcomes, and in some cases, neighborhood factors have the same impact as a student being economically disadvantaged (a well-established predictor of academic success). Botting shared a map of Tulsa that shows to what extent neighborhoods have a positive or negative impact on student outcomes (see Figure 6-3).

The neighborhood patterns found by the CEI are quite similar to the patterns found using the Opportunity Atlas. This means, said Botting, that education data paired with neighborhood data are an early indicator of

DATA INFRASTRUCTURE FOR STUDYING MOBILITY 73

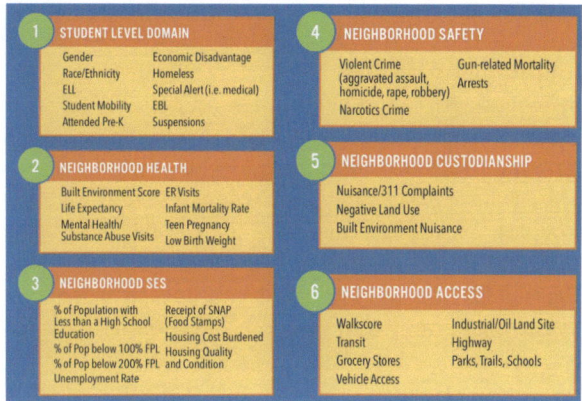

FIGURE 6-2 Child Equity Index data.
NOTE: ELL = English language learner; EBL = emergent bilingual learner; ER = emergency room; FPL = federal poverty level; SES = socioeconomic status; SNAP = Supplemental Nutrition Assistance Program.
SOURCE: Workshop presentation by Daniel Botting, February 15, 2022.

social mobility. This not only makes the issue of social mobility more accessible to constituents, but it also enables researchers and policy makers to intervene early and to test the impact of these interventions. As anyone who has worked in education or politics knows, said Botting, there is a strong desire to get immediate results and "little patience" for programs that take years to bear fruit. Pairing these data can show the value of community investment in shorter-term educational outcomes and longer-term social

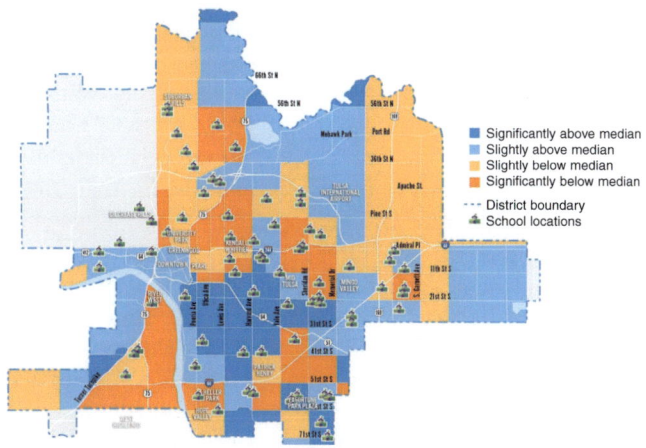

FIGURE 6-3 Child Equity Index map of Tulsa.
SOURCE: Workshop presentation by Daniel Botting, February 15, 2022.

mobility. In addition, the CEI can be used to inform policy decisions such as the busing of students, school vouchers, and other interventions aimed at changing educational outcomes.

While pairing education and neighborhood data has great potential for research and action, said Botting, there have also been challenges. First, getting the data is difficult. Educational data are held by individual school districts, and many of these do not have the resources, funding, or time to pull the data themselves. Neighborhood-level data come from many different sources and different levels, including counties, cities, police departments, hospitals, and county health systems. Bringing together these multiple data sources was "time-consuming and difficult," and there is a need to streamline the accessibility and usability of these data. Another challenge is a lack of consistent longitudinal data collection in education. Tests are constantly changing, he said, and the tests cannot always be compared with one another. Furthermore, data may vary across state lines or even district lines, with different categorization of characteristics such as race and ethnicity.

Botting closed by sharing side-by-side maps of historical redlining, the CEI, and the Opportunity Atlas, and noted that the patterns in Tulsa have remained similar for decades. The same neighborhoods are "good" or "bad" in each map, showing both the persistence and the root of the problem. Many of today's inequalities, said Botting, stem from racist policies and systems of the past. "This doesn't even begin to capture" the impact of major events such as the Tulsa race massacre, in which a White mob attacked and destroyed Black neighborhoods. Mobility is generational, said Botting, and the use of educational and neighborhood data can help researchers begin to understand and address some of the root causes.

Household Financial Data

The JPMorgan Chase Institute, said Fiona Greig, uses administrative data from the firm's banking records to try to understand what is happening in the economy and with families. These data are de-identified, and include a variety of information such as balances, credit card activity, mortgages and home equity loans, individual transactions, and demographic characteristics. These data have a number of advantages, said Greig. The large sample sizes can offer insight into distributional, geographic, and other sub-group variation. High frequency longitudinal data are available on a range of outcomes, and the data are adaptable to changing economic and policy environments. Greig walked workshop participants through three examples of ways in which banking data can be used to study social mobility: the evolution of household cash balances during COVID-19, income growth during business cycles, and understanding the sources and consequences of racial wealth gaps.

Evolution of Household Cash Balances During COVID-19

National data show that cash balances and liquid balances have grown during the COVID-19 pandemic, said Greig, but it is less clear from such data how this phenomenon played out for different types of families. The institute, which continually updated and published data to understand how different income groups fared over time, found that federal fiscal supports had a large impact, particularly for low-income families (see Figure 6-4). Median cash balances through September 2021 remained elevated for families, and there were significant jumps at each round of federal help.

Income Growth During Business Cycles

Greig's second example focused on how macroeconomic environments and policies play into matters of inequality. Comparing the rates at which household incomes grew by income quartile between 2013 and 2021, Greig explained that after the Great Recession, high-income families experienced faster income growth than low-income families, but by the time the pandemic hit, this pattern had reversed (see Figure 6-5). At the same time, however, substantial downward income changes before the pandemic were most common among low-income households. The next step, said Greig, is

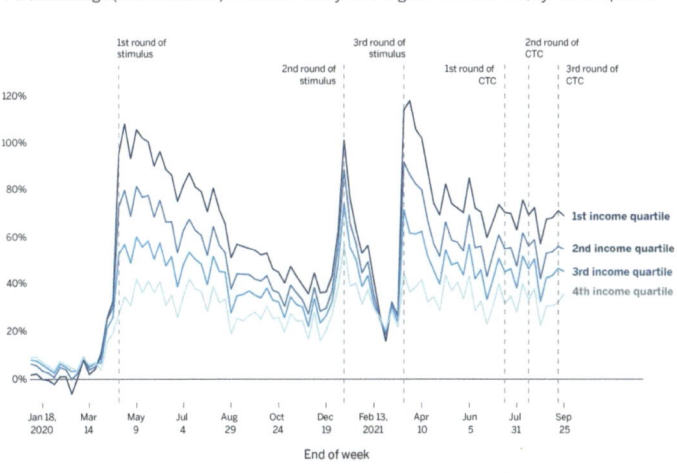

FIGURE 6-4 Median cash balances, January 2020–September 2021.
SOURCE: Workshop presentation by Fiona Greig, February 15, 2022.

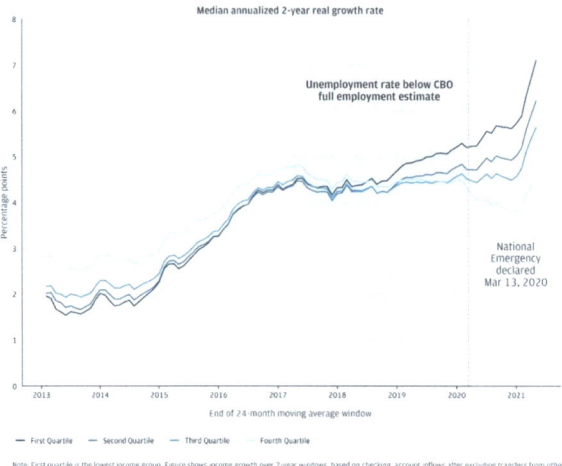

FIGURE 6-5 Income growth through business cycles, 2013-2021.
NOTE: CBO = Congressional Budget Office.
SOURCE: Workshop presentation by Fiona Greig, February 15, 2022.

to extend and examine these types of dynamics with other outcomes, such as wealth balances, refinancing, and home purchasing.

Understanding the Sources and Consequences of Racial Wealth Gaps

The share of families who have student loan debt has grown tremendously over the last couple of decades, said Greig. Black families are disproportionately likely to have debt; around 30 percent of Black families hold some sort of educational loan. Compared with White and Hispanic borrowers, Black borrowers are less likely to be making progress on their student loans, with sizable percentages either making no payments or on track to never pay off the loan. By pairing credit bureau data with checking account data, said Greig, it became clear that loan repayment is a "family affair." Nearly 40 percent of individuals who are making student loan payments are doing so on someone else's behalf (e.g., spouse, child, parent). Looking at this phenomenon by race, Black and Hispanic individuals were less likely than White individuals to either give or receive help in paying down student debt. This emphasizes the intergenerational nature of debt, said Greig; an individual borrows money for school because their family lacks the ability to pay, and then is also less likely to receive help in repayment.

DATA INFRASTRUCTURE FOR STUDYING MOBILITY

Another racial difference that can be explored with banking data, said Greig, is the impact of job loss on spending. The institute looked at the extent to which families reduced their spending when a family member lost a job involuntarily (pre-pandemic). Overall, there is a significant drop in consumption, she said, but there is a much larger drop among Black and Hispanic families compared with White families (see Figure 6-6). These differences can be explained by racial gaps in liquid and financial assets, which serve as buffers during times of income loss.

In closing, Greig compared administrative data with government survey data, noting that their comparative advantages and disadvantages underscore their value as a complement to one another (see Figure 6-7). For example, administrative data tend to have large sample sizes, whereas government surveys have small sample sizes. On the other hand, government data tend to have representative samples, whereas administrative data require using benchmarking to assess representativeness.

DATA GOVERNANCE

There are competing goals for the data held by federal statistical agencies, including survey, census, and administrative data, said Katharine Abraham (University of Maryland, College Park). The data need to be made available in order to inform decisions, but there is also a need to protect the privacy of data subjects. The challenge, she emphasized, is to develop models for data infrastructure and data access that best serve both goals. Abraham described two models for data infrastructure. The first is a data warehouse, in which data assembled from different sources are permanently housed in a single

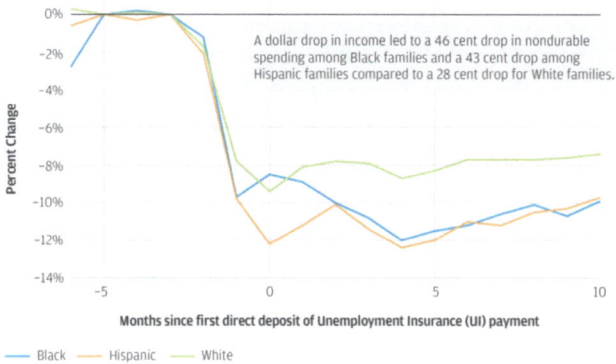

FIGURE 6-6 Changes in non-durable spending after job loss.
SOURCE: Workshop presentation by Fiona Greig, February 15, 2022.

Administrative Data	Government Data
✓ **Large samples** offer insight into distributional and subgroup variation	✗ **Small samples**, challenged by low response rates
✓ **High-frequency, longitudinal nature**	✗ **Snapshots at a low frequency**
✓ **Adaptable** to changing policy and economic environment	✗ **Difficult to change** survey instruments "on the fly"
✓ Observe **revealed preferences based on actual transactions**	✗ **Survey responses** subject to respondent interpretation and recall bias
✗ **Samples** require benchmarking to assess representativeness	✓ **Representative samples**
✗ Data are a **byproduct of operations** that • can change over time • require design choices to map to real world concepts or units	✓ **Survey design** can ensure comparability • between observations over time • to measures in other datasets

FIGURE 6-7 Comparative advantages of administrative and government data.
SOURCE: Workshop presentation by Fiona Greig, February 15, 2022.

location. The second is a data facility, in which core data are permanently housed in a single location and data needed for specific projects are brought in as needed but not permanently retained. In its final report, the Commission on Evidence-Based Policymaking recommended a data facility rather than a data warehouse. While not storing data permanently complicates the ability to replicate and extend prior analyses, Abraham said, there are concerns about the real and perceived privacy risks of the data warehouse model.

There are also different models for data access and dissemination. Federal agencies make data available in a variety of ways, including published tabulations, publicly available microdata files, and confidential microdata files available through the Federal Statistical Research Data Centers and other agencies. Abraham said that she "can't emphasize enough" how much progress has been made in the past 20-25 years with respect to making data available to researchers while protecting privacy. Statistical agencies are required by law to protect data subjects, and different methods are used to do so. For microdata, methods include coarsening categorical variables, top-coding continuous variables, noise infusion, and data swapping. For tabular releases, approaches include cell suppression, noise infusion, swapping in underlying microdata, and cell value rounding. The exact methods used are not generally made public. Privacy considerations also govern the release of research results generated behind the statistical agency firewall.

There is a growing recognition, Abraham said, that the privacy protection methods applied historically may be inadequate. The typical statistical disclosure methods are not as private as they seem; a determined hacker may be able to glean confidential information from existing releases. Abraham warned that if there were a breach of promised privacy protections, the surrounding publicity could have "very negative consequences" for the federal statistical system. In order to address these weaknesses, the U.S. Census Bureau has begun to adopt disclosure avoidance methods based on differential privacy. Use of these methods is not yet widespread but Abraham expects that it will grow. An implication of these increased privacy protections, said Abraham, is that there will be decreased access to microdata in the form of public use files.

In order to ensure that researchers retain access to necessary data, there will be a need for a new access and dissemination model. This model, said Abraham, could use a tiered access system in which users work with synthetic data to run their models, and then have the results checked against data behind the firewall to verify whether the results are reasonable. If this initial step is unsuccessful, the researcher could apply for access to the original data behind the firewall. For this model to work, however, there need to be changes such as a more streamlined process for applying for microdata access, expanded access capacity, and improved capacity to evaluate the privacy implications of proposed data releases.

Some initial steps have been taken toward a new model for access and dissemination, said Abraham. The Foundations for Evidence-Based Policymaking Act of 2018 directed the creation of standardized data access procedures, and established an Advisory Committee on Data for Evidence Building; the committee is considering an implementation plan for a National Secure Data Service (i.e., a data facility). Moving forward, said Abraham, difficult questions related to privacy will need to be addressed. The two major issues, in her view, are creating a balance between privacy and access and how the "privacy budget" will be allocated. The differential privacy methods being used by the U.S. Census Bureau give a way to characterize the tradeoff between privacy and access, but the question of the balance is a policy question, not a technical one. Each release of information uses up some of the "privacy budget," and there need to be conversations about the implications of decisions made, as well as what data are highest priority for release. One way to answer these questions, Abraham suggested, could be to establish a review committee that would guide what projects are undertaken.

Abraham said that as a researcher, she is not "particularly happy" that data may become more difficult to access. In conversations such as this workshop, however, it is important to consider not just what data are available but also the privacy implications of making data available. Abraham said that she is "optimistic" privacy protections can be strengthened while preserving the value of the data, but that it will be a challenge.

DISCUSSION

Following the presentations, C. Matthew Snipp (Stanford University) moderated a discussion with the speakers and workshop participants.

Tension between Access and Confidentiality

Snipp opened by reflecting on the history of social science research within the federal government. Over the past 50 years, there has been a "historic devolution" in the government's capacity for conducting basic social research, he said. According to Snipp, agencies today barely have the capacity to conduct research or plan operations; for example, the U.S. Census Bureau struggled to conduct tests of new systems that were planned for the 2020 Census. During this period, there has been growing reliance on outside researchers, and initiatives that encourage researchers to access federal data and to share data across agencies. However, at the same time, there have been growing concerns about privacy and confidentiality of federal data, particularly Census data. These concerns have resulted in new policies and practices, such as differential privacy, in order to protect data. Given the tension between confidentiality of the data and the importance of conducting social research, Snipp asked speakers to comment on how they think this tension will be resolved.

Abraham began by recalling a previous U.S. Census Bureau director who believed that the U.S. Census Bureau "didn't have any business doing basic research;" to the contrary, Abraham said it is critical for agencies that produce data to also conduct research. If there are not people at the agency working with the data, they are not going to fully understand the data they are collecting, she said. Fortunately, there is "significant research" going on at all of the agencies, but the idea that they should not be conducting research persists. Genadek agreed that the U.S. Census Bureau is currently very supportive of both external and internal researchers, and that innovative research tools—such as linked data infrastructure—are being created with the full support of the U.S. Census Bureau and other government agencies.

Regarding the tension between confidentiality and access, Abraham continued, the laws are very strict and the agencies have little wiggle room. Some of the laws may not seem to make sense, but these protections are a policy decision rather than an agency decision. Greig agreed that there is a constant tension between access and privacy, and said that "not a day goes by" that JPMorgan Chase Institute is not asked for access to their data. For example, the institute has discussed the possibility of publishing spending data that could be added into national statistics. While this seems possible, she said, what seems impossible is committing to doing this over time on a continual basis. One challenge is that the aggregation standards applied to data in order to protect privacy may have to change over time; for example, if there is a big shift in retail activity to specific retailers, the whole series of data needs to be re-aggregated. This creates temporal comparison challenges if the application of the standards results in different levels of aggregation over time.

Agency Cooperation

There is a great deal of valuable data held by the federal government, said Fabian Pfeffer (University of Michigan). For example, the U.S. Census Bureau population data—particularly if linked with other data—have the potential to greatly advance research on mobility and racial inequalities. Pfeffer asked speakers to comment on the potential for cooperation between agencies, and between agencies and outside researchers, given concerns about privacy. Abraham said that new approaches to privacy do have the potential to restrict how and what data get released; for example, estimates might be released with more noise infused, or certain data may not be released at all. The issue of agencies working with one another is very important, she said, and there may be a need to revisit the structure of the federal statistical system. When agencies produce statistics based on surveys designed for that purpose, "it didn't really matter" that the agencies were separate entities. With the increasing use of administrative data and nontraditional sources of data, however, it has become more important to coordinate and systematize the research efforts of various agencies.

Confidentiality Versus Granularity

Earlier in the workshop, Jennifer Lee (Columbia University) discussed the need for granularity in data in order to capture the heterogeneity in the Asian American population. Such approaches as differential privacy, said Snipp, can "seriously distort" small areas and small populations. Snipp asked Abraham whether there is middle ground between confidentiality and granularity. "I am not sure that there is," Abraham replied. There is noise in the data already, and differential privacy makes the data noisier, but there may not be a solution because of the legal constraints. Abraham suggested that reconsidering what type of data need to be kept confidential could be a solution, but this is not possible under the current rules.

Potential for Combining Multiple Data Sources

A workshop participant wondered if there was a "parallel universe" in which all of the data from the projects presented in this session could be integrated. "We could evaluate the outcomes in the Tulsa kids using the decennial data, or look at their spending at JPMorgan," he said, and asked panelists for their thoughts. Genadek responded that this is a "definite possibility." The U.S. Census Bureau has a history of bringing in data from researchers, and facilitates the provision of these data to other researchers. However, she said, the proprietary nature of data and the different rules around them make sharing challenging. "It's a beautiful vision" to see all these data together, but it may not be possible in the near future. Botting replied that Impact Tulsa would love the opportunity to bring in data from other sources to help them get new details and new insight into what is happening in a child's life. For example, Botting said, the data they use now only classifies a child as "economically disadvantaged" or "not economically disadvantaged." Being able to see if the household had a bank account with $1 or $10,000 would be extremely useful. Greig said that the JPMorgan Chase Institute is actively exploring the possibility of collaborating with outside data providers, but there are a few challenges and questions that first need to be answered. Specifically, who is responsible for keeping data secure, what are the boundaries on who else can use the data, and what is the purpose of the collaboration? If these challenges can be addressed, said Greig, the opportunity is obvious and the potential for impact is very clear.

Botting shared an example of how Impact Tulsa was able to make a difference during the pandemic. When schools went virtual, many students did not have reliable internet access. Impact Tulsa served as an intermediary to pair data from school districts with data from local internet providers to identify students who needed internet. The schools were then able to reach out and provide them with a hot spot or city-sponsored internet. This is a "bright spot" that shows what can be done with "a lot of work and a lot of commitment."

How to Improve Local Data

Snipp asked Botting to elaborate on how local data could be improved—specifically, how to ensure more consistency to facilitate longitudinal research. Commitment and investment from the state is critical, responded Botting. If state agencies choose to change the tests used, they could choose to make it possible to compare the tests with each other, but this takes money. Researchers need to make sure that politicians and state educational agencies understand that having longitudinal data is valuable so that they are willing to invest in the tools that make it possible, he concluded.

Most Critical Needs

Snipp asked speakers to briefly identify their top priorities for data or methods that could advance the study of social mobility. Ideas included the following:

- Data that link generations and are paired with identifiers around race and other characteristics. (Greig)
- Data that examine spending patterns and the implications for welfare. (Greig)
- Linked Census data. (Genadek)
- Consistent state-level education data with a streamlined process for gaining access. (Botting)

7

Moving Forward: The Role of Policy and Key Takeaways

Throughout the workshop, speakers and participants touched on how research can support the development of good policies, and the role that policy plays in either facilitating or inhibiting mobility. To bring these discussions together, Wendy Edelberg and Bob Greenstein (Brookings Institution) held a "fireside chat," in which they explored existing policies that impact mobility, what types of policies might be most effective moving forward, and how to best translate research findings into policy. To close out the workshop, Courtney Coile (Wellesley College) asked planning committee members to identify key takeaways from the discussions and to share their thoughts on where the field should go from here.

THE ROLE OF POLICY

In this session, Edelberg and Greenstein engaged in a back-and-forth conversation with each other and with workshop participants about the role of policy in reducing income inequality and poverty, and in increasing inter- and intragenerational upward mobility. Edelberg began by emphasizing the importance of upward mobility for policy makers. "History shows us that people with financial means will always find ways to protect themselves and work for the success of their children," she said, and one of the highest priorities for government is to ensure that those opportunities are available to all people, regardless of financial circumstances.

Most Critical Policies for Children

Edelberg asked Greenstein to identify the policies that can best ensure that a child's circumstances do not "determine their destiny," and asked him to comment on how these types of interventions and programs could be made more effective. Greenstein responded by focusing on two areas of policy, the child tax credit and housing policies, which hold potential to improve mobility for children, though he stressed that these were not the only important policies.

Child Tax Credit

There is a strong evidence base to support the notion that providing a fully refundable child tax credit on an ongoing basis could enhance children's life chances and promote mobility, said Greenstein. A fully refundable credit, he said, ensures that low-income families get the full amount because it is not tied to the level of parental income. Some policy makers have argued that providing cash assistance via the child tax credit could substantially discourage work among the poorest families. Greenstein disagreed with this idea but said that political debate on this point has made it a "front and center" topic in social policy. In 2021, a fully refundable child tax credit was in effect due to the pandemic, but it is unclear what will happen in the future. Further research in this area has real potential to impact policy outcomes in the years ahead, he said.

Housing Policy

Housing has a big impact on children's well-being, Greenstein continued, including adverse effects from evictions and housing instability. Interventions in this area can make a difference, as was demonstrated by a study which found that children under 13 in families that used a voucher to move to a lower-poverty, higher-opportunity area experienced improved mobility.[1] This evidence led the U.S. Partnership for Mobility from Poverty to propose that vouchers be provided to low-income families with young children, and that the vouchers be accompanied by intensive mobility services to help families navigate issues and succeed in moving to a new lower-poverty neighborhood. This proposal has not become law, but Congress has appropriated money for a demonstration project that will begin soon. This is another area, said Greenstein, where further research could provide

---

[1] Chetty, R., Friedman, J.N., Hendren, N., Jones, M.R., and Porter, S.R. 2018. *The Opportunity Atlas: Mapping the Childhood Roots of Social Mobility.* NBER Working Paper No. 25147. Cambridge, MA: National Bureau of Economic Research.

more data on the impacts of this type of approach, and could improve understanding of which housing mobility strategies are more or less effective.

Human Capital Investments

Greenstein asked Edelberg to talk about human capital investments that can promote mobility—and in particular, the role of fiscal policy in securing or incentivizing those investments. There are a range of programs that support human capital investments, she said, including those that support early childhood education; student loan programs; and efforts to protect workers, such as paid leave and closing the wage gap. Ensuring access to high-quality early childhood education, she said, is a "no-brainer." Head Start and Early Head Start aim to reduce poverty by providing comprehensive preschool programs to meet the emotional, social, health, nutritional, and psychological needs for children from low-income families. However, only around 36 percent of eligible children ages 3-5 and only 11 percent of eligible children under age three had access to these programs in 2020. These numbers are "far too low," she said, given the evidence linking the programs to positive short- and long-term impacts, including reducing the intergenerational transmission of poverty. More research, including long-term research, is needed in order to build the evidence base necessary to increase support from policy makers.

The government also invests in workforce development programs, such as training and reemployment for displaced and disadvantaged workers. Evidence for the effect of specific programs is mixed, she said, but evidence shows that the more successful programs are those that focus on specific populations and sectors. This is a "critical place" to increase data and research, she said. Another area ripe for research is in the area of workers' bargaining power and how it can support upward mobility. At this moment in time, said Edelberg, the balance of power has shifted, and workers are able to demand more pay and better working conditions. However, whether this continues remains to be seen. The government can do more to support workers' rights to unionize; it is clear that unions lift wages, reduce inequality, and shape how work is organized. Workers in certain industries—such as agriculture and warehousing—have less bargaining power, and research could help document this phenomenon and support policies to address it.

Lasting Policies

With policy work, said Edelberg, "there is no point at which we declare victory." A policy that is in place has no guarantee of remaining in place forever, she continued, then asked Greenstein to discuss how to make policies "stick." He responded that there is a tension between having policies stick and having the most effective policies. A recent book by Eric Patashnik[2] examines what types of policy reforms get reversed, and what types persist through changes in government. One insight from the book, said Greenstein, is that a policy enacted on a purely partisan basis is more likely to be reversed than one that had a lot of bipartisan support when first enacted. For example, if a fully refundable child tax credit were to be enacted this year in a Congress controlled by Democrats, he said, it is likely that Republicans would try to repeal full refundability if they regain control. Patashnik also makes the observation that policies can become embedded over time as they develop a constituency. For example, it would be much more difficult for Republicans to repeal the Affordable Care Act now than it was several years ago.

While evidence supporting the effectiveness of a policy matters, it is not definitive; Greenstein said, "simply showing that something is effective doesn't mean you are going to get the political support to enact it, but it definitely helps." He gave an example of congressional debate on the Special Supplemental Nutrition Program for Women, Infants, and Children (WIC). WIC is targeted to low-income families, but was only serving a fraction of the eligible population because there was not enough funding. Evidence of its efficacy was accruing, and at a congressional hearing, a panel of Fortune 500 CEOs testified that WIC was the "health care equivalent of a triple-A rated investment." In the months that followed, there was a bipartisan commitment that Congress would appropriate enough money each year so that all eligible families who applied could receive the benefit. This is an example, he said, of how the evidence of impact can really matter. The chances of enacting a policy such as the refundable child tax credit would be "materially enhanced" if new research could demonstrate positive mid- and long-term effects on children and insignificant effects on parental employment.

Work Requirements

A number of the social policies aimed at improving upward mobility contain work requirements, said Edelberg. One argument often made in favor of work requirements is that people's participation in the labor force is an essential ingredient to creating upward mobility. However, evidence suggests that work requirements do not have the desired effect of meaningfully increasing people's participation in the labor force; Edelberg said this is a critical area where researchers can contribute evidence to impact policy making. Greenstein agreed that more research is needed in this area, and

---

[2]Patashnik, E. 2008. *Reforms at Risk: What Happens After Major Policy Changes Are Enacted*. Princeton, NJ: Princeton University Press.

posited that some work requirements are effective in incentivizing employment while others are not. There is evidence that the Earned Income Tax Credit increases employment, and some research suggests that the employment-increasing effects of the credit are a significant poverty reducer.[3] Other types of work requirements—such as those in Medicaid programs—seem to be ineffective. Citing evidence from the Arkansas Medicaid program, Greenstein said these requirements appear to have little noticeable effect on employment but have a major effect on people becoming uninsured or unable to access needed benefits. While the courts have struck down work requirements for Medicaid, there is reason to believe that work requirements will continue to be a major focus of debate in the social program structure. This is another area, he said, in which more research could make a significant impact on policy making.

Translating Evidence into Policy

Kathleen Mullan Harris (University of North Carolina at Chapel Hill) recalled that earlier in the workshop, Greg Duncan (University of California, Irvine) noted that an understanding of the processes of mobility does not necessarily equate to an understanding of what types of policies should be enacted to impact mobility. Harris asked Edelberg and Greenstein to comment on how research findings can be better translated for policy makers. Edelberg referred to the Hamilton Project[4] as an example of a place that does such work. Its core mission, she said, is to reach out to academics and experts and help them translate their findings for a policy audience; the Hamilton Project helps academics go beyond simply including a section on "policy implications," and make the policy implications and their policy ideas more concrete and actionable. Greenstein offered another perspective, saying that academic researchers who are not familiar with the political process should not strive to "go beyond what they know." When researchers do have a significant sense of policy implications, he said, they can and should spell them out for the reader. He encouraged researchers to acknowledge any uncertainty on the details of the policy implications, but to "make what contribution" they can.

Greenstein noted that an academic paper may not be the ideal place for researchers to reach policy makers, because of the structure, style, and audience for these papers. A better approach may be to issue a policy brief that accompanies the academic paper; he noted that many research centers engage in this practice. Partnerships with organizations such as the Hamilton Project

---

[3] Hoynes, H. 2019. The earned income tax credit. The ANNALS of the American Academy of Political and Social Science, 686(1), 180-203.

[4] https://www.hamiltonproject.org/

or the Center on Budget and Policy Priorities can also be useful for researchers hoping to make an impact on policy discussions. These organizations can work to connect researchers with policy makers, and can facilitate fruitful conversations between the two. He said that there are people in Washington who are "happy to help" make the connection between the people doing the research and the people making the policy. Finally, Greenstein said that engaging university communications staff can help draw attention to research findings; "often it takes getting one journalist" to take an interest and "all of a sudden you're in the middle of the policy debate."

Differing Goals of Policies

Policies in this area, said Coile, can look similar but be directed at different goals, such as reducing poverty, reducing inequality, or increasing social mobility. Coile asked Edelberg and Greenstein to give their perspectives on these different goals and how they think about the tradeoffs between types of policies. Edelberg responded that these goals are generally overlapping, but some policies, such as those directed at helping people suffering from a temporary setback, are aimed at reducing shorter-term inequality. For example, if a certain segment of the population experiences a dramatic decrease in income during a recession, the government may provide temporary assistance to ensure that they can weather the storm. These policies are directed at inequality rather than long-term mobility, but "of course they are totally related." Greenstein said that discussions of mobility have often treated the "ladder" and the "safety net" as if they are entirely separate things. One of the key developments in recent years, he said, has been evidence that significant poverty reduction, especially in early childhood, affects long-term mobility. However, there is still not widespread understanding among policy makers about this relationship between the safety net and the ladder, and public education is this area is an important need.

KEY TAKEAWAYS

At the end of the workshop, Coile asked the planning committee members to share their thoughts on the key points made and insights provided, needs that were identified, issues that may have been missed, and implications for policy.

General Observations on Social Processes and Structures

Planning committee members shared some of the key observations they made over the course of the workshop. Several members spoke about the centrality of the family unit in mobility; for example, Snipp said that Greig's data about family members paying back student loans underscored the importance of family. Logan said researchers need to look at how families have changed over time and how these changes impact mobility. A great deal of research has focused on family form and how families function as an economic unit; this research should be incorporated into measures of mobility. Mobility is "essentially a family process," said Harris, and data and theories should reflect this relationship. Harris also emphasized the importance of considering mobility as a life course process. The life course looks different for different cohorts, different populations, and at different times, she said, and people acquire human, financial, and social capital at different times across their life course. Methods for measuring and understanding mobility should consider and capture these differences.

Small noted the importance of structures and institutions. He highlighted Sharkey's discussion of how policies and institutions create boundaries and space that separate neighborhoods in ways that impact mobility, and he recalled Lee's discussion of trust and underreporting and how understanding of the Asian American experience is enhanced as a result of people's understanding of governing institutions. Small also said that integrating research on structures, including structural racism, is critical for understanding mobility. Coile agreed, recalling Brown's observation that the ability to understand the effects of structural racism has been hampered by the current inability to measure it. Coile said that she also agreed with Brown's call for creating a public data resource on measures of structural racism, which could be used by other researchers to help explain outcome measures.

Need for New Data, New Models, and New Theories

Many planning committee members identified the need for new data, new models, and new theories in order to drive the field of social mobility forward. Snipp noted that there has not been a major sociological study of social mobility since the 1970s. This may be one reason for the dearth of major methodological innovations in quantitative sociology, he said; although there have been many tweaks to existing methodologies, there have not been revolutionary developments along the lines of the introduction of path analysis of the log linear models in the 1970s. However, the lack of a comprehensive study has also led to increased interest in the area and new efforts to create data infrastructure and data linkages—the importance of which, Snipp said, was "impossible to overstate." Recalling the discussion from the data infrastructure session, Snipp said that some parts of the federal government wanted to make data more available while others wanted to restrict access; who will prevail in this disagreement will not be up to the social scientists or even to the agencies, as this is ultimately an issue that will have to be settled either in the courts or in Congress. Coile agreed with Snipp that while there is substantial promise on the data front, there are also challenges in terms of access and privacy, as well as tensions inherent in the fact that private companies collect data for purposes other than research. Snipp reminded the workshop participants about the National Academies consensus study underway on "The Scope, Components, and Key Characteristics of a 21st Century Data Infrastructure"[5]; the study will explore the possibility of developing a consistent set of standards across all federal statistical sources, think about ways of incorporating data from the private sector and state and local governments, and so on.

Harris identified several future needs for mobility research. She said there is a need for more research on topics including subjective social status (in addition to components and forms of mobility such as education, income, occupation, and wealth), the timing of investments, and the interaction between individuals and structural systems (e.g., educational, legal, criminal justice, and health care). Harris emphasized the importance of data on wealth, which she said can be difficult to get but for which there are some good extant sources in terms of home ownership, residence, and credit information; she recalled Darity's comment on the importance of getting information on the wealth of parents and grandparents, which would be more difficult to get. Intergenerational data are also a particularly major need, according to Harris, and this can be addressed by adding simple questions to surveys (e.g., place of birth for the individual, the parent, and the grandparent; citizenship; and nativity) or through data linkages projects. Recalling the presentations by Brown and Sharkey, Harris said that researchers are making good progress on structural measures by being "incredibly entrepreneurial and resourceful," and there is a need to build infrastructure to make these data available to all. Finally, said Harris, many speakers emphasized the importance of qualitative data and the importance of integrating qualitative data within quantitative studies.

Snipp and Coile concurred with the need for more qualitative data. Coile added that she observed a need for data that allows researchers to see variation in smaller areas and groups. Recalling Small's presentation, she pointed out the need for hyperlocal data on places (e.g., at the block level), as well as the need to be able to adopt a broader comparative approach and compare across areas. Coile said that it is also important to have the data necessary to understand the experiences of subgroups (e.g., different ethnicities within the larger group of Asian Americans).

While acknowledging the data needs, Small said that "data alone can't produce science." Given the vast amount of data that are and will become

---

[5] https://www.nationalacademies.org/our-work/the-scope-components-and-key-characteristics-of-a-21st-century-data-infrastructure-a-workshop

available, he said, new theoretical ideas and models can be developed to increase understanding of mobility. Logan agreed with Small, saying that "some of our mobility research has been too guided by the data" and noting the importance of thinking theoretically about the real meaning of mobility and how it can be measured accurately. Logan added that there are currently many ways to define and think about mobility—for example, occupational, wealth, and income mobility—and a theory that can integrate these different types and examine the relationship between them is needed.

Harris recalled the integrative model that Grusky presented and said that this is "a goal that mobility research should aspire to." At the same time, there is a need to identify and explore the complexities of a model of mobility; as with any type of integrative model, she said, "you just sort of chip away at it." Coile agreed with Harris and indicated that the conversation about the integrative model was "an exciting development." Coile also said that the "convergence" across the fields of sociology and economics was a welcome development, both with regard to causality and the greater attention being paid to models, theory, institutions, and contextual factors.

What May Have Been Missed

Members identified a number of issues that either were not discussed at all or received only a brief mention. Pfeffer noted that some issues were deliberately excluded from the workshop in the interest of time, but that these issues would be important to explore in future conversations. International perspectives were not well represented during the workshop, said Pfeffer, and there is a lot to learn from other countries. Another area for future exploration is the intersection between gender inequalities and social mobility; although Lee reported interesting findings on gender at the intersection of race and ethnicity, this is a topic that has lagged behind and deserves more empirical research. Finally, said Pfeffer, the distinction between social mobility and social inequality was touched on a few times, but further conversation would be useful to explore the relationship between mobility and inequality, and how "in a society where the rungs of the ladder are further apart, it is harder to climb the rungs."

Logan pointed out that there were many discussions of policy at the workshop, but few mentions of politics. Politics is inextricably linked to mobility, he said; the distribution of resources, the places people live, and where investments are made are all political issues. For example, cities that were very segregated in the 19th century made the first early investments into water systems; choices about how to exclude some people from clean water resulted in persistent racial differences in waterborne diseases. On the other side, said Logan, research shows that families who were enslavers at the end of the Civil War maintained their economic position after the end of slavery; this phenomenon is a function of power and the political process. There is a political and historical process that "makes place good and makes place bad," said Logan, and one cannot talk about the importance of place without talking about the impact of politics on place. In discussions of mobility, Logan said it is important to bring politics more fully into the conversation, and to clearly articulate what it means for policy and programs.

Snipp said that not much was heard during the workshop about the importance of social media and what can be learned from those resources. He indicated that, to his knowledge, not much thought has been given to how those data might be used to learn about social mobility; however, network models and the kinds of things on which those data are being brought to bear might have some promise and may be worth thinking about in the future.

Informing Policy

Small said he was struck by the distinction in Duncan's presentation between problem research and program research. There has been great progress on problem research—that is, understanding the phenomenon of social mobility—and the future is "even more promising than I thought," he said. However, program research—knowing what to do—has been more limited and there is space for much more work in the future. Researchers can design or evaluate ideas that are part of the policy conversation, he said, but more importantly, they can contribute to the discourse and identify the questions that should be asked.

Edelberg made three points about how research can inform policy. First, she said, there is a need for clarity about what is meant by "mobility." The word *mobility* is often used to refer only to upward mobility; there are a number of policies designed to give people the opportunities and the resources necessary to move up the mobility ladder. However, policies designed to improve mobility can also be directed at making the rungs on the ladder closer together and potentially moving people at the top of the distribution down. According to Edelberg, "the rules have been rigged" in such a way that the children of wealthy parents stay wealthy. She said that policies need to remove unfair advantages (e.g., legacy preferences in college admissions), and the conception of mobility needs to include not only pulling people up from the bottom of the distribution but also seeing people at the top of the distribution move down. Edelberg explained that this distinction is important for two reasons. First, there are different policies that can be more or less successful along each of these lines. Second, this distinction is the reason why people sometimes talk at cross purposes regarding whether or not the United States has more or less mobility than other countries, or more or less mobility now than it used to.

The second point about policy that Edelberg made was the importance of considering and researching the most basic questions. She noted that policy debates often center around questions that researchers may consider ill-informed or simplistic (e.g., do policies without work requirements encourage people to stay poor?). By taking these questions seriously and providing straightforward answers, Edelberg said that researchers can shift the policy discourse, provide answers to those who want them, and provide "cover" to policy makers who are being confronted with ill-informed arguments. Finally, said Edelberg, the battle for good policy is never won. Because policies can be repealed, it is important to remain vigilant: "we will never just unfurl the banner saying: 'Mission Accomplished.'"

CLOSING OF THE WORKSHOP

Upon the conclusion of the discussion, Coile and Majmundar thanked the planning committee members, the speakers, and the workshop participants for their work and input. In addition, Coile thanked the Gates Foundation for their support of the workshop, and the staff at the National Academies for their work in putting the workshop together. Coile adjourned the workshop.

Appendix A

Workshop Agenda

Workshop on Strengthening the Evidence Base to Improve Economic and Social Mobility in the United States

February 14-15, 2022

> Inequalities in income, wealth, health, and life expectancy have been increasing over the last several decades in the United States. Since around 1980, fewer Americans than before are doing better than their parents did—that is, more are experiencing downward socioeconomic mobility in terms of occupational status and income. A number of efforts are currently under way to develop evidence-based strategies for increasing inter- and intra-generational mobility and improving economic and social well-being in the United States. These efforts require an improved understanding of the factors that influence social and economic mobility, the mechanisms through which these factors operate, and how these relationships and mechanisms vary across and within different population subgroups. The purpose of this workshop is to identify key research and data needs and priorities for future work on social and economic mobility. After the workshop, the National Academies Press will publish a rapporteur-prepared proceedings volume that summarizes the workshop presentations and discussions.

DAY 1: MONDAY, FEBRUARY 14, 2022

11:00-11:20 am ET	**Welcome and Goals for Workshop** • *Malay Majmundar*, Director, Committee on Population • *Kosar Jahani*, Bill & Melinda Gates Foundation • *Courtney Coile*, Wellesley College (Chair, Workshop Steering Committee)
11:20 am-12:50 pm	**Social and Economic Mobility: State of the Field**
11:20-11:35 am	Setting the stage: Introduction to social and economic mobility • *Deirdre Bloome*, Harvard University
11:35-11:50 am	Key findings from sociology and future directions in mobility research • *David Grusky*, Stanford University
11:50 am-12:05 pm	Key findings from economics and future directions in mobility research • *Joseph Ferrie*, Northwestern University
12:05-12:15 pm	Moderator/discussant questions and reflections • *Courtney Coile*, Wellesley College
12:15-12:50 pm	General Discussion
12:50-1:10 pm	**BREAK**
1:10-3:00 pm	**Conceptual Approaches and Frameworks for Studying Mobility**
1:10-1:25 pm	Causal inference and mobility • *Jennie Brand*, University of California, Los Angeles
1:25-1:40 pm	Exploring the relationship/reducing the disconnect between studying inter- and intra-generational mobility • *Xi Song*, University of Pennsylvania

1:40-1:55 pm	Interventions to increase mobility: Conceptual issues • *Greg Duncan*, University of California, Irvine
1:55-2:10 pm	The potential of qualitative and ethnographic research • *Mario Luis Small*, Columbia University
2:10-2:20 pm	Moderator/discussant questions and reflections • *Fabian Pfeffer*, University of Michigan (Member, Workshop Steering Committee)
2:20-3:00 pm	General Discussion
3:00-3:20 pm	**BREAK**
3:20-5:00 pm	**Research Priorities and Data Needs for Studying the Spatial Dimensions of Mobility**
3:20-3:35 pm	Research priorities for place-based investments • *Matthew Staiger*, Harvard University, Opportunity Insights
3:35-3:50 pm	Challenges and opportunities for studying mobility in urban areas • *Patrick Sharkey*, Princeton University
3:50-4:05 pm	Challenges and opportunities for studying mobility in rural areas • *Daniel Lichter*, Cornell University
4:05-4:10 pm	Moderator/discussant questions and reflections • *Mario Luis Small*, Columbia University (Member, Workshop Steering Committee)
4:10-5:00 pm	General Discussion
5:00 pm	**Adjournment**

DAY 2: TUESDAY, FEBRUARY 15, 2022

11:00 am-1:00 pm ET	**Research Priorities and Data Needs for Studying Mobility by Race, Ethnicity, and Immigration Status**
11:00-11:15 am	Challenges and opportunities for studying mobility by race and ethnicity • *William ("Sandy") Darity*, Duke University
11:15-11:30 am	New multilevel data and measures of structural racism/institutional discrimination • *Tyson Brown*, Duke University
11:30-11:40 am	Moderator/discussant questions and reflections • *Trevon Logan*, The Ohio State University (Member, Workshop Steering Committee)
11:40-11:55 am	Challenges and opportunities for understanding mobility and the immigrant experience • *Tomás Jimenéz*, Stanford University
11:55 am-12:10 pm	Challenges and opportunities for understanding mobility among Asian Americans • *Jennifer Lee*, Columbia University
12:10-12:20 pm	Moderator/discussant questions and reflections • *Kathleen Mullan Harris*, University of North Carolina at Chapel Hill (Member, Workshop Steering Committee)
12:20-1:00 pm	General Discussion
1:00-1:20 pm	**BREAK**
1:20-2:00 pm	**Policy, Poverty, and Upward Mobility**
1:20-1:35 pm	"Fireside Chat" between • *Robert Greenstein*, Brookings Institution • *Wendy Edelberg*, Brookings Institution (Member, Workshop Steering Committee)

APPENDIX A

1:35-2:00 pm	General Discussion
2:00-3:50 pm	**Data Infrastructure for Studying Mobility**
2:00-2:15 pm	The use of administrative data to study mobility • *Katie Genadek*, U.S. Census Bureau
2:15-2:30 pm	Challenges and opportunities regarding data governance • *Katharine Abraham*, University of Maryland, College Park
2:30-2:45 pm	The use of non-traditional data sources (school district data/student data) to study mobility • *Daniel Botting*, Impact Tulsa
2:45-3:00 pm	The use of non-traditional data sources (household financial data) to study mobility • *Fiona Greig*, JPMorgan Chase Institute
3:00-3:10 pm	Moderator/discussant questions and reflections • *C. Matthew Snipp*, Stanford University (Member, Workshop Steering Committee)
3:10-3:50 pm	General Discussion
3:50-4:10 pm	**BREAK**
4:10-5:00 pm	**Key Themes and Next Steps to Move the Field Forward**
5:00 pm	**Adjournment**

Appendix B

Biographies of Planning Committee Members and Presenters

KATHARINE G. ABRAHAM (Presenter) is distinguished university professor of economics and survey methodology at the University of Maryland, College Park. Her published research includes papers on the contingent workforce, the work and retirement decisions of older Americans, unemployment and job vacancies, and the measurement of economic activity. Abraham is an elected member of the American Academy of Arts and Sciences, a distinguished fellow of the American Economic Association, and a fellow of both the American Statistical Association and the Society of Labor Economists. She has a Ph.D. in economics from Harvard University.

DEIRDRE BLOOME (Presenter) is professor of public policy at the Harvard Kennedy School and faculty member at the Harvard Center for Population and Development Studies. Her current research focuses on a demographic approach toward investigating how patterns of social inequality are produced and reproduced. Bloome's prior work focused on the relationships among socioeconomic inequality, mobility, and insecurity; the historical evolution of racial inequalities in the family and economy; and statistical methods for characterizing population heterogeneity. She has received multiple awards including The William Julius Wilson Early Career Award from the American Sociological Association's Inequality, Poverty, and Mobility section. Bloome has a Ph.D. in sociology and social policy from Harvard University.

DANIEL BOTTING (Presenter) is a senior data analyst at Impactful, a collective impact organization that uses data to drive systemic change across the cradle to career continuum, with the goal that all children in Tulsa have every opportunity to succeed. Botting has an M.A. in public policy and applied economics from the University of Michigan.

JENNIE E. BRAND (Presenter) is professor of sociology and statistics at the University of California, Los Angeles (UCLA). She is also director of the California Center for Population Research and co-director of the Center for Social Statistics at UCLA. Brand serves as chair of the Inequality, Poverty, and Mobility Section of the American Sociological Association (ASA). She was elected to the Sociological Research Association in 2019, and received the ASA Methodology Leo Goodman Mid-Career Award in 2016. She also serves as a member of the Technical Review Committee for the National Longitudinal Surveys Program at the Bureau of Labor Statistics. Brand is associate editor of *Science Advances*. Her research focuses on social stratification and inequality, and its implications for various outcomes that indicate life chances. Brand holds a Ph.D. in sociology from the University of Wisconsin–Madison.

TYSON BROWN (Presenter) is associate professor of sociology at Duke University, inaugural presidential fellow, and director of the Center on Health and Society. His program of research examines the *who*, *when*, and *how* questions regarding racial inequalities in health and wealth. Brown has authored numerous articles in leading sociology, population health and health policy journals, and his research contributions have been recognized with awards from the American Sociological Association. He is currently working on several projects that address fundamental questions about racial stratification by conceptualizing, measuring, and mapping structural racism, as well as quantifying its impact on the life chances. Brown serves on the board of directors of the Population Association of America, as well as on the editorial boards of several journals, including *Demography*, *Social Forces*, and the *Journal of Health and Social Behavior*. He has a Ph.D. in sociology from the University of North Carolina at Chapel Hill.

COURTNEY C. COILE (Chair of Planning Committee) is professor of economics at Wellesley College. She is also a research associate of the National Bureau of Economic Research (NBER), where she serves as co-director of the NBER Retirement and Disability Research Center and co-director of the International Social Security project. Coile's research focuses on the economics of aging and health, with particular interests in retirement decisions, health trends, and public programs used by older and disabled populations. She is co-author of *Reconsidering Retirement: How Losses and Layoffs Affect Older Workers*, and co-editor of the *Social Security Programs and*

Retirement Around the World series. She is a current member of the National Academies' standing Committee on Population. Coile has a Ph.D. in economics from the Massachusetts Institute of Technology.

WILLIAM DARITY JR. (Presenter) is Samuel DuBois Cook professor of public policy, African and African American studies, and economics, and director of the Samuel DuBois Cook Center on Social Equity at Duke University. Previously, he served as chair of the Department of African and African American Studies and was founding director of the Research Network on Racial and Ethnic Inequality at Duke. Darity's research focuses on inequality by race, class, and ethnicity; stratification economics; schooling and the racial achievement gap; North-South theories of trade and development; skin shade and labor market outcomes; the economics of reparations; the Atlantic slave trade and the Industrial Revolution; the history of economics; and the social psychological effects of exposure to unemployment. Darity has a Ph.D. in economics from the Massachusetts Institute of Technology.

GREG DUNCAN (Presenter) is distinguished professor in the School of Education at the University of California, Irvine. His recent work focuses on estimating the role of school-entry skills and behaviors on later school achievement and attainment and the effects of increasing income inequality on schools and children's life chances. Duncan is part of a team conducting a random-assignment trial assessing impacts of income supplements on the cognitive development of infants born to poor mothers in four diverse U.S. communities. He was elected to the National Academy of Sciences in 2010. He has a Ph.D. in economics from the University of Michigan.

WENDY EDELBERG (Planning Committee Member) is director of The Hamilton Project and a senior fellow in economic studies at the Brookings Institution in Washington, DC. She also serves as principal at WestExec Advisors. Most recently, Edelberg was chief economist at the Congressional Budget Office. She worked on issues related to macroeconomics, housing, and consumer spending at the President's Council of Economic Advisers during two administrations. Before that, she worked on those same issues at the Federal Reserve Board. Edelberg is a macroeconomist whose research has spanned a wide range of topics, from household spending and saving decisions, to the economic effects of fiscal policy, to systemic risks in the financial system. She has a Ph.D. in economics from the University of Chicago.

JOSEPH FERRIE (Presenter) is professor of economics and history at Northwestern University, where he has taught since 1991. He is also a research associate at the National Bureau of Economic Research. Ferrie's research focuses on intergenerational economic and social mobility and the later-life impacts of early-life economic and environmental circumstances. His work has appeared in the *American Economic Review*, the *Journal of Political Economy*, and the *Quarterly Journal of Economics*. He is the author of *Yankeys Now: Immigrants in the Antebellum U.S. 1840-1860* (Oxford University Press, 1999). Ferrie has a Ph.D. in economics from the University of Chicago.

KATIE R. GENADEK (Presenter) is director of the Decennial Census Digitization and Linkage (DCDL) project at the U.S. Census Bureau. The DCDL project includes digitizing images of the 1960-1990 Censuses, capturing information from the images, and linking these data into the U.S. Census Bureau's Data Linkage Infrastructure. Genadek also works on supporting research through the Federal Statistical Research Data Centers by documenting and disseminating the U.S. Census Bureau's linked data. She previously worked at the University of Minnesota, where she managed the IPUMS-USA data project and directed the outreach efforts for all IPUMS data projects. Genadek is a demographer and economist, and her research is focused on the relationship between policy, work, family, and time use. She holds a Ph.D. in applied economics from the University of Minnesota.

ROBERT GREENSTEIN (Presenter) is a visiting fellow in economic studies at the Brookings Institution, where he is affiliated with The Hamilton Project. He is founder and president emeritus of the Center on Budget and Policy Priorities. Greenstein was appointed by President Clinton in 1994 to serve on the Bipartisan Commission on Entitlement and Tax Reform and headed the part of President Obama's transition team that dealt with the federal budget. His work has focused on the federal budget and programs and policies affecting people with low or modest incomes, on which he has written extensively. In 1996, he was awarded a MacArthur fellowship for making "the Center a model for a non-partisan research and policy organization." Greenstein was elected to the American Academy of Arts and Sciences and received the Daniel Patrick Moynihan prize from the American Academy of Political and Social Science, which cited him as "a champion of evidence-based policy." He has an A.B. from Harvard University.

FIONA GREIG (Presenter) is managing director and co-president at the JPMorgan Chase Institute, which delivers data-rich analyses and expert insights for the public good. She joined the Institute in 2014 after serving as deputy budget director for the City of Philadelphia. Greig previously served as a consultant for McKinsey & Company and in 2009 she started and ran Bank on DC, a financial inclusion program for the District of Columbia. She has published research on topics including household finance, health care, labor markets and the Online Platform Economy, gender, and behavioral decision making. Greig has a Ph.D. in public policy from Harvard University.

DAVID B. GRUSKY (Presenter) is Edward Ames Edmonds professor in the School of Humanities and Sciences, professor of sociology, senior fellow at the Stanford Institute for Economic Policy Research, faculty fellow at the Center for Population Health Sciences, director of the Stanford Center on Poverty and Inequality, co-editor of *Pathways Magazine*, and a member of the American Academy of Arts and Sciences. His research addresses such topics as trends in inequality, poverty, and mobility in the United States; new approaches to reducing poverty and increasing mobility; and new data infrastructures for monitoring trends and crises and evaluating interventions. Grusky has a Ph.D. in sociology from the University of Wisconsin–Madison.

KATHLEEN MULLAN HARRIS (Planning Committee Member) is James E. Haar distinguished professor of sociology, adjunct professor of public policy, and faculty fellow at the Carolina Population Center at the University of North Carolina at Chapel Hill. Her career has focused on social inequality and health with particular interests in health disparities, biodemography, sociogenomics, and life course and aging processes. Harris served as director and principal investigator of the National Longitudinal Study of Adolescent to Adult Health (Add Health). Her recent research has examined the health effects of despair, isolation, and stress; social genetic effects; health costs of upward mobility; and the obesity epidemic and young adult health. She was awarded the Golden Goose Award from the U.S. Congress in 2016 for major breakthroughs in medicine, social behavior, and technological research. Harris is an elected member of the National Academy of Sciences and the American Academy of Arts and Sciences and an elected fellow of the American Association for the Advancement of Science. She has a Ph.D. in demography from the University of Pennsylvania.

TOMÁS JIMÉNEZ (Presenter) is professor of sociology and comparative studies in race and ethnicity at Stanford University. He is also director of the undergraduate program on urban studies. His research and writing focus on immigration, assimilation, social mobility, and ethnic and racial identity. Jiménez's forthcoming book, *States of Belonging: Immigration Policies, Attitudes, and Inclusion,* uses survey data and in-depth interviews to understand how state-level immigration policies shape belonging among Latino immigrants, U.S.-born Latinos, and U.S.-born Whites in Arizona and New Mexico. He has published his research in *Science, American Sociological Review, American Journal of Sociology, Proceedings of the National*

Academy of Sciences, Social Problems, International Migration Review, and many others. He has a Ph.D. from Stanford University.

JENNIFER LEE (Presenter) is Julian Clarence Levi professor of social sciences at Columbia University. Her wide-ranging research addresses morally urgent questions about the implications of contemporary U.S. immigration—particularly Asian immigration—on the native-born population. Lee is a board member of the Obama Presidency Oral History, a trustee of the Russell Sage Foundation, and a senior researcher at AAPI Data, which recently received a $10 million grant to study anti-Asian discrimination and hate. Committed to public engagement, Lee is a contributor for *Science* and the Brookings Institution, and has written for *The New York Times*, *The Washington Post*, *Los Angeles Times*, and other media outlets. She was recently invited by the Biden-Harris Administration to present her research on xenophobia, discrimination, and anti-Asian hate to COVID-19 Health Equity Task Force. She has a Ph.D. in sociology from Columbia University.

DANIEL T. LICHTER (Presenter) is Ferris Family professor emeritus of life course studies in the Department of Policy Analysis and Management at Cornell University. Lichter has published widely on topics such as population and public policy and for over four decades he has centered much of his work on the changing social and economic conditions of rural America. His most recent work has focused on rural depopulation over the past century, and on fertility and reproductive health in small-town America. He has provided new national estimates of racial residential segregation in Hispanic "boom towns" in the Midwest and South, focusing on the spatial assimilation and economic incorporation of the new immigrants into local communities. Lichter's most recent paper *A Demographic Lifeline to Rural America: Latino Population Growth in New Destinations, 1990-2019* was published in *Investing in Rural Prosperity* by the Federal Reserve Bank of St. Louis in 2021. He has a Ph.D. in sociology from the University of Wisconsin–Madison.

TREVON D. LOGAN (Planning Committee Member) is Hazel C. Youngberg trustees distinguished professor of economics and associate dean in the College of Arts and Sciences at The Ohio State University. He also serves as a research associate in the Development of the American Economy Program and director of the Race and Stratification in the Economy Working Group at the National Bureau of Economic Research. Logan is currently co-director of the American Economic Association's Mentoring Program and a member of the editorial boards of the *Journal of Economic Literature* and the *Journal of Economic Perspectives*. His current research focuses on racial inequality and economic history. He is currently a member of the National Academies' planning committee on Strengthening the Evidence Base to Improve Economic and Social Mobility in the United States and a current member of the National Academies' Committee on Population. Logan has a Ph.D. in economics from the University of California, Berkeley.

FABIAN T. PFEFFER (Planning Committee Member) is associate professor and associate chair of the Department of Sociology and research associate professor at the Institute for Social Research at the University of Michigan. He also serves as director of the Center for Inequality Dynamics and as a co-investigator of the Panel Study of Income Dynamics. Pfeffer's research investigates social inequality and its maintenance across generations and time. Current projects focus on wealth inequality and its consequences for the next generation, social mobility across multiple generations, the maintenance of inequality through education, and the effects of experiencing social mobility. He is the recipient of the Early Career Award from the American Sociological Association's section on Inequality, Poverty, and Mobility and the section on Sociology of Education. Pfeffer has a Ph.D. in sociology from the University of Wisconsin–Madison.

PATRICK SHARKEY (Presenter) is William S. Tod professor of sociology and public affairs at the Princeton University Woodrow Wilson School of Public & International Affairs. Sharkey was formerly chair of sociology at New York University, served as scientific director at the Crime Lab in New York, and was the founder of AmericanViolence.org. He has a Ph.D. in sociology and social policy from Harvard University.

MARIO LUIS SMALL (Planning Committee Member) is Grafstein family professor in the Department of Sociology at Harvard University. Small's published work focuses on urban poverty, personal networks, and the relationship between qualitative and quantitative methods. He is currently studying the relationship between networks and decision-making, the ability of large-scale data to answer critical questions about poverty, and the role qualitative inquiry in cumulative social science. Small has authored numerous books, including *Villa Victoria: The Transformation of Social Capital in a Boston Barrio* and *Unanticipated Gains: Origins of Network Inequality in Everyday Life*. He currently serves as the University of Bremen excellence chair and as a board member of International Network for Social Network Analysis. Small is an elected member of the American Academy of Arts and Sciences. He has a Ph.D. in sociology from Harvard University.

C. MATTHEW SNIPP (Planning Committee Member) is Burnet C. and Milfred Finley Wohlford professor of sociology at Stanford University. He has written extensively on American Indians, focusing specifically on the interaction of American Indians and the U.S. Census. Prior to moving to Stanford, Snipp was associate professor and professor of rural sociology at the University of Wisconsin–Madison, where he held affiliate appointments with several other units, and assistant and associate professor of sociology at the University of Maryland. He has also served on the U.S. Census Bureau's Racial and Ethnic Advisory Committee and on the Board of Scientific Counselors for the U.S. Centers for Disease Control and Prevention/ National Center for Health Statistics. A current member of the National Academies' Committee on National Statistics, he has served on numerous National Academies panels including the Panel on Research on Future Census Methods (2010 planning), Panel on Residence Rules in the Decennial Census, Panel to Review the 2010 Census, and the Standing Committee on Reengineering Census Operations. Snipp has a Ph.D. in sociology from the University of Wisconsin–Madison.

XI SONG (Presenter) is associate professor of sociology and demography at the University of Pennsylvania. Her research interests include social stratification and mobility, inequality, population studies, and quantitative methodology. Song's research has demonstrated the values of genealogical microdata for studying long-term family and population changes. As a quantitative methodologist, she developed Markov chain demography models for genealogical processes, multivariate mixed-effects location-scale models for the interplay of inequality generating process across life stages and generations, population estimation for overlapping generations and kinship network, and weighting methods for reconciling prospective and retrospective mobility estimates. Song has a Ph.D. in sociology from the University of California, Los Angeles.

MATTHEW STAIGER (Presenter) is research scientist at Opportunity Insights. His research investigates the determinants of economic opportunity with the goal of identifying policies that would be effective at promoting upward mobility. During graduate school, he participated in the Pathways Internship at the U.S. Census Bureau and was a dissertation scholar at the Washington Center for Equitable Growth. He has a Ph.D. in economics from the University of Maryland.